WINEMAKING WITH ELDERBERRIES

WINEMAKING WITH ELDERBERRIES

("*The British Grape*")

T. Edwin Belt

WINEMAKING WITH ELDERBERRIES

Published by:
"The Amateur Winemaker" Publications Ltd.,
South Street, Andover, Hants. SP10 2BU

1st Impression 1981

ISBN 0 900841 62 1

Printed in Great Britain by:
Standard Press (Andover) Ltd.,
South Street, Andover, Hants. SP10 2BU

CONTENTS

COMPARE IT

Nutritionally the elderberry is way ahead even of that superb fruit which is always held to be ideal for winemaking, the grape. You find that incredible? Then compare the nutritive values

GRAPE

Botanical information: The fruit of the grapevine of any one of the many species of the genus *Vitis*, cultivated for eating and for making wine and raisins.

Nutritive values:

Vitamin A: 80 I.U. per 100 gm.
Vitamin B: Thiamine 0.06 mg.;
  Riboflavin 0.04 mg.; Niacin 0.2 mg.
Vitamin C: 4 mg.
Protein: 1.4 gm.
Calories: 70

Fat: 1.4 gm.
Carbohydrates: 14.9 gm.
Calcium: 17 gm.
Iron: 0.6 mg.
Phosphorus: 21 mg.

Reported health benefits: Grapes are called "the queen of fruits" because of their great internal body cleansing properties. A good blood and body builder, it is a source of quick energy. Grape juice is easily assimilated and called the "nectar of the gods." It is indicated in cases of constipation, gout and rheumatism, skin and liver disorders. This alkaline fruit helps greatly to decrease the acidity of the uric acid and lends itself further in aiding the elimination of the acid from the system, thus benefiting the kidneys greatly.

WITH THE GRAPE!

of the two fruits' constituents, as set out by JOSEPH M. KADAUS in his "Encyclopaedia of Medicinal Foods" (Thorsons Publishers Ltd., Wellingborough, Northants).

ELDERBERRY

Botanical information: Purple-black drupaceous fruit of the common elder (genus *Sambucus*).

Nutritive values:

Vitamin A: 600 I.U. per 100 gm.
Vitamin B: Thiamine 0.07 mg.;
Riboflavin 0.06 mg.; Niacin 0.5 mg.
Vitamin C: 36 mg.
Protein: 2.6 gm.
Calories: 72

Fat: 0.5 gm.
Carbohydrates: 16.4 gm.
Calcium: 38 mg.
Iron: 1.6 mg.
Phosphorus: 28 mg.

Reported health benefits: Elderberries are recommended in cases of bronchitis, sore throats, coughs, asthma, colds, catarrh, and constipation. They also induce perspiration.

Preparation: The most common use of elderberries is in the making of wine and jelly.

Elderbush in full bloom.

INTRODUCTION

The Common Elder, which is widespread in the British Isles and in North America, produces black-violet and green-coloured berries in profusion, which are excellent for winemaking purposes; indeed, a can labelled 'grape concentrate' once purchased by myself undoubtedly included a proportion of elderberry juice with its contents. It made an excellent, quick-fermenting wine, but when these berries are free for the garnering it is sounder economics to purchase a reputable grape concentrate and add your own proportion of elderberry juice.

A fast fermentation is characteristic of the elderberry, and impatient winemakers can be as happy in its use as with the commercial 'quickie' wines, given the same temperature control and a good wine yeast. I have had elderberry table wines ferment out in twelve days.

The advantages of the elderberry and elderflower for winemaking are: that it is probably alone with the grape in making superb wines from aperitif through table, sparkling table, and social to dessert, and from red to rosé and white wines; it is quickly and easily gathered from thornless, low-hanging branches; no fruit demands so little of the gardener as to site, soil, or attention, and it is decorative as a tree, shrub or hedge; it is pest-free, needing no spraying, is very easily propagated, and will bear fruit within eighteen months of a cutting being planted.

The other main ingredients used in the recipes are to be obtained ready for use from supermarkets and the corner shop, thus reducing the work involved to the minimum. This does not mean that the enthusiastic winemaker is precluded from using fruits fresh from the tree or bush, of course.

HISTORY & LEGEND

There is a saying that one can consume the whole of a pig apart from the squeal – this may not be entirely correct, but the early herbalists certainly held a broadly similar view so far as the use of the elder tree or bush is concerned.

Present-day herbalists still avail themselves of the attributes of the elder, and the whole subject is seen in true perspective when it is appreciated that the aspirin (the modern premier pain-killer for millions of rheumatic sufferers the world over), is a synthetic version of the acid found in the bark of white willow, which the early herbalists used for that same purpose.

The 17th century herbalist Nicholas Culpeper had this to say about the elder (Sambucus nigra):

"Government and Virtues – This is under the dominion of Venus. The first shoots of the Common Elder boiled like asparagus, and the young leaves and stalks boiled in fat broth, do mightily carry forth phlegm and choler. The middle or inward bark boiled in water, and given in drink works much more violently; and the berries, either green or dry, expel the same humour, and are often given with good success to help the dropsy; the bark of the root boiled in wine, or the juice thereof drank, works the same effects, but more powerfully than either the leaves or fruit. The juice of the root taken, mightily procures vomitings, and purges the watery humours of the dropsy. The decoction of the root taken, cures the bite of an adder, and bites of mad-dogs. It mollifies the hardness of the mother, if women sit thereon, and opens their veins, and brings down their courses; the berries boiled in wine, perform the same effect; and the hair of the head washed there-with, is made black. The juice of the green leaves applied to the hot inflammations of the eyes assuages them; the juice of the leaves snuffed up into the nostrils, purges the tunicles of the brain; the juice of the berries boiled with honey, and dropped into the ears, helps the pains of them; the decoction of the berries in wine being drunk, provokes urine; the distilled water of the flowers is of much use to clean the skin from sun-burning, freckles, morphew, or the like; and takes away the head-ache, coming of a cold cause, the head being bathed therewith. The leaves or flowers distilled in the month of May, and the legs often washed with the said distilled water, takes away the ulcers and sores of them. The eyes washed therewith, it takes away the redness and blood-shot; and the hands washed morning and evening therewith, helps the palsy, and shaking of them."

Culpeper's contemporary, the learned Dutch physician Dr. Boerhaave, never passed an elder tree without raising his hat in its honour, so the saying goes.

The Germans, too, superstitiously raised their hats when passing an elder tree or bush.

Herbalists are not the only people who have been concerned in the very long history of the elder. It was the subject of folklore in Denmark, where it was thought to be under the protection of the 'Elder Mother,' whose permission was required (how this was to be obtained is not clear) before one gathered the flowers. It was taboo to use the elder in the construction of household furniture, particularly cradles, since a baby put into an elder cradle would be strangled by the 'Elder Mother' (this may have connections with modern 'cot-deaths.').

From the practical standpoint, elder is a corruption of eller, meaning a Saxon kindler, who used the hollowed stems as a blowpipe-cum-bellows, and its botanical name, Sambucus, is of ancient Greek origin, the Greek sambuke being the name of a musical pipe made from hollowed elder stem.

The wood of the elder has been used to make kegs, skewers, and mathematical instruments for generations, but the days seem to have gone when children made themselves pea-shooters and whistles from shoots with the pith removed.

Boretree, the north-country name for the elder, derives from the ease of removal of the pith from the stems.

The cross is said to have been made from elder wood, and according to legend Judas hanged himself on an elder – the mushroom-like excrescences on the bark are still known as Judas's (or Jews') ears.

Elderberry trees are often found near old cottages, since it was considered to be unlucky to destroy them, and hedgers still superstitiously sometimes refuse to cut them.

Herbalists of the 20th century, like their country-wise contemporaries, regard elderberry wine as a good drink for the treatment of the common cold and influenza, and on the continent of Europe the juice of elderberries is favoured for the relief of rheumatism and sciatica.

To stop a cold, induce perspiration, and relieve the symptoms of bronchitis, elderberry rob (thick jam) is said to be effective. This is made by simmering 2.27 kg. (5 lb.) of elderberries with 453 g. (1 lb.) of sugar and the juice of 2 lemons until it thickens, when it is strained and bottled. The dosage is 2 tablespoonfuls in hot water not exceeding 74°C (165°F), together with a tablespoonful of whisky. If hotter water is used, you will vapourise the alcohol in the whisky, which seems to be an awful waste of money!

Elderflower tisane (tea) has a reputation for the relief of the common cold and influenza, and is also sleep-inducing, encourages perspiration, and "increases the flow of urine." It is made by brewing a teaspoonful of the dried flowers in a cupful of boiling water for 5 minutes, straining, and sweetening to taste; if left to grow cold, a delightful muscatel-flavoured summertime refresher results. Elderflower teabags can be bought in health food shops.

A tisanes made from the dried leaves is best made with one teaspoonful per cup, infused for 5 minutes – here again the quantity to use is finally a matter of taste.

Elderflower water relieves inflammation of the eyes, eases sunburn, softens the skin with daily use, is a mild astringent, and removes freckles and wrinkles, so it is still said, though perhaps this is a hand-down from Culpeper.

Chilblains can be treated with elderflower ointment, made in the same manner as leaf ointment.

The berries yield a dye, which has been used as a hair-dye; they are also useful as a laxative.

The bruised leaves will keep insects away, and are used in healing ointment. This is made by simmering the young leaves in lard, adding enough leaves to make the lard 'as green as grass,' after which it is strained, cooled and potted in an airtight jar, ready for the treatment of inflammations.

The inner bark of the tree is purgative and emetic in large doses.

Warts are said to be cured by rubbing with elder, and there is probably a connection between this cure and the elder's supposed protection against witchcraft in earlier times. However, the writer lost a wart some years ago by burying a piece of meat in the garden, so comment is superfluous; in that case the wart was rubbed with the meat, of course.

There are other traditional uses of the elder:

Elderberry sauce is made by pouring 568 ml. (one pint) of boiling vinegar over 568 ml. (one pint) of elderberries contained in an oven dish, and leaving covered overnight at minimum oven heat; then put the sieved-off liquor into a saucepan with a teaspoonful of salt, a sliver of mace, 40 peppercorns, 12 cloves, a finely chopped onion and a modicum of ginger, and simmer for ten minutes; bottle complete, and mature for at the least 18 months.

As a substitute for ice cream soda, try munching the fresh flowers on a hot summer's day.

A muscatel flavour is given to gooseberry jam when 4 flower heads, without stalks, to each 453 g. (pound weight) of gooseberries is contained in a muslin bag and boiled with the fruit.

Elderflower heads dipped in batter and deep fried, after which the main stalk is cut off, are a delicacy when served with sugar.

Elderberries are a tasty addition when making apple pies, and are often added to blackberry jelly in the making.

Elderberry jelly (the connoisseur's delight) is made by baking the berries slowly in the oven until soft, pouring into a jelly bag and leaving to drip overnight, covered. Allow the juice to run out without squeezing the bag, add the juice of one lemon for every 907 g. (2 lb.) of the fruit used, followed by 453 g. (1 lb.) of sugar for every 568 ml. (pint) of juice, and simmer until setting point is reached.

CLASSIFICATION & CULTIVATION

The Caprifoliaceae or honeysuckle family did well to produce an offspring called Sambucus, or the elder, and in particular the Sambucus nigra (having black-violet berries) and the Sambucus nigra virescens (having green berries), which can be made into the whole gamut of quality wines. In common with the grape, different varieties of the elder produce various types of wine, and these varieties will now be described:

Sambucus nigra – the elder, common elder, mealy tree, or whitewood, is a deciduous shrub or tree which is native to England, and was introduced to Ireland, southern Scotland and Wales. It grows in woods, waste places and hedges. A fertile, fresh to damp, chalky soil is favourable to good growth, especially if the tree is also in a sunny place, but the elder will withstand some shade and a poorish soil. It is an irregularly branched shrub or tree; will grow to a height of 9 m. in favourable circumstances. The crooked stem and branches have a core of white pith; the fissured bark is pale brown, corky and fragile. In winter the twigs are grey-green in colour, with pairs of reddish buds along them. The rather dull yellow-green, or dark green leaves are about 15 cm. long, are composed of a number of distinct segments or leaflets which succeed each other along the mid-rib, usually 5 to 7 in number, each being broad, tapered to a point at either end, regularly and sharply toothed, almost smooth, the underside covered with grey hairs; each about 3 cm. across and 7 cm. long. The flowers are white or cream-coloured, each about 5 mm. across, and appear in much-branched, flat-topped, disc-like clusters, sometimes containing 200 blooms, and each about 16 cm. across.

The fruits are a shiny, black-violet colour when ripe, passing from pale green through crimson, and are about 5 mm. in diameter; each contains 2 or 3 small flattened stones. Sucker shoots emerge from the base of the shrub in some profusion. If you see leaves opening from the buds of a shrub or tree in January, you are most likely examining an elder, which is the earliest shrub thus to remind us that spring is coming. The whole tree has a narcotic and unpleasant smell; the flowers have a bitter scent; they contain a volatile oil, tannins, gum, glycoside, choline, and vitamins. The flowers are harvested in May, June and July; they bloom from the outside of the cluster inwards, and should be picked for wine-making when the inner ones have all opened, but before the outer ones are full-blown. They must be collected with care to avoid bruising, otherwise they will turn black when being dried; they can, of course, be used fresh. Avoid heaping the flowers for the journey home, otherwise they will heat up and again be spoilt for drying purposes. The forenoon or evening of a dry day is the best time for harvesting.

The leaves are also used fresh or dried and are collected in the two months of June and July. The berries ripen in September and October. They are best picked in the bunch and can be separated from the stalks by means of a dinner fork. They can be used fresh, or preserved in a variety of ways, as described in "Preserving Winemaking Ingredients". The root is dug up in October.

Sambucus nigra virescens can be recognised by its white bark, and the fruits are pale green to straw-coloured when fully ripe, with green, gooseberry-like stripes; the stones can be seen through the skin.

There are other varieties of the black-violet berried Sambucus nigra, and this offers a choice of either garnering the berries without regard to their type (which is quite satisfactory when they are being used with other fruit), or keeping the harvest from each tree or bush separate, and having an elderberry connoisseur's selection of wines. These varieties can be recognised as follows:

Sambucus nigra albovariegate (marginata or argenteomarginata) has leaflets with an irregular, creamy-white edge.

Sambucus nigra aurea has golden-yellow leaflets which darken in the autumn.

Sambucus nigra aureomarginata has an irregular bright yellow leaf margin.

Sambucus nigra heterophylla (linearis) has variable-form leaflets.

Sambucus nigra laciniata has finely divided leaflets reminiscent of the fern and parsley.

Sambucus nigra pulverulenta has leaflets mottled and striped white.

Sambucus nigra aurea.

Sambucus nigra purpurea has leaflets flushed purple.
Sambucus nigra rotundifolia has round leaflets.
Sambucus nigra pyramidalis is recognisable by the inverted pyramid, erect shape of the tree.
Sambucus nigra plena has double flowers.

There is also another variety of Sambucus nigra which is suitable for white wines:
Sambucus nigra fructuluteo whose fruits are yellow, and which is more common than the green variety, although my own white winemaking has been with the rarer type, since I had ready access to a very prolific specimen near our former home.

There are various species of elderberry in the United States of America, for it is a very popular winemaking fruit over there, and grown on a large scale commercially. Some of these are to be found in Britain. The parent variety, the American or sweet elder, is:

17

Sambucus canadensis, which has purple-black fruit, grows into a large tree, has 5 to 11 but usually 7 leaflets per leaf, and white flowers in convex heads 13 to 20 cm. (5 to 8 in.) across, which bloom in July.

Others of this family are:

Sambucus canadensis maxima, which can be recognised by the rosy-purple flower stalks carrying flower heads 30 cm. (12 in.) across. The leaves are up to 45 cm. (18 in.) long.

Sambucus canadensis sub-mollis has greyish leaflets having soft down on their underside.

Sambucus canadensis caerulea has blue fruit with a white bloom on it.

There are several varieties of red and scarlet-fruited elderberries which have not found popularity in the winemaking world, and need not be discussed here, since the colour of the fruit makes them readily recognisable.

However, there is one variety of the elder which is unsafe for winemaking, and a description of this is essential:

Sambucus ebulus, dwarf or ground elder, or Danewort, grows on waste ground, having stout, grooved, annual stems which grow to about one metre (3 ft.) in height. The leaves encompass 9 to 13 leaflets. The pinkish-white flowers grow in groups of three, blossoming in July and August, and their flattened hairy heads are about 9 cm. (3½ in.) across. The fruit is black, unfortunately similar to Sambucus nigra, but fortunately this strongly purgative promoter of the secretion and flow of urine does not regularly come to fruition, whereas the Sambucus nigra is very bounteous.

There are several local names for our native Sambucus nigra, and these can be of assistance when making enquiries in unfamiliar country districts:

Bourtree, Boretree or *Bottary*; Ches. Lincs. Lancs. Yks. Lakes.
Dur. Northum. S.Scot. N.Ire.
Borral; Northum. S.Scot.
Bulltree; Cumb.
Devil's wood; Derb.
Dogtree; Yorks.
Eller; Suss. Kent. Norf. Ches. Derby. Lincs. W.Yorks. N.Engl.
God's stinking tree; Dor.
Judas-tree; Kent.
Scaw; Corn.
Teatree; Som.
Trammon; IoM.

If you have a garden, however small, you can easily grow your own elderberries, even if this means planting the bush in a hedge. Elders are not fussy in their growing requirements.

It is suggested that, to be sure of producing single-fruit wine to your taste, berries from different trees and bushes should be harvested, making a careful note of the source of each batch of berries, then when the wines have been sampled you will be in a position to take a cutting from the tree or bush of your choice. The differences in taste may not be marked, but 'if a job is worth doing, it is worth doing well', and it is to be hoped that you will have many years of drinking your home-grown and home-made wine ahead of you. Some elderflowers do not have the pleasant bouquet required for winemaking, and some exploration on this account is advisable.

Seeds of the elder are available from nurserymen, but they are not produced for their winemaking value, and it is far better to take cuttings from a favoured winemaking tree or bush.

The cuttings are taken either trom young shoots in July/August or from the ripened current year's growth in the autumn, the cut being made with a secateur just below a leaf node, to give a length of about 30 cm. (12 in.) for planting. The cut end is then dipped in hormone rooting material, and the cutting buried about 15 cm. (6 in.) deep. Fruit may be produced as early as the second year. Incidentally, it has been found that the best berries are carried on wood which is one year old, which indicates that pruning to bush form rather than tree form will be advantageous, particularly as suckers grow readily; but if you do not bother to prune, you can still expect a bounteous crop from the elder. The elder will grow in dry soil, but moist and fertile ground produces the more luscious berries; it is a good competitor for the available food in the soil.

The flowers harvested from your own garden can be collected quite easily without detriment to the succeeding fruit, since a close watch can be kept to catch them when full-blown, and not before. The method then is to hold a container positioned to catch the petals as they are lightly brushed off from the flower heads with the flat of the hand.

There is again an advantage when gathering garden-grown berries, since it is again readily practicable to choose the best time for harvesting them – fully ripe fruit makes, by far, the best wine. The berries are not quite ready when they have all turned black-violet in colour – they are not ripe for winemaking until they are soft and easily squashed by the fingers; this last applies also to the green variety, our *Sambucus nigra virescens*. Secateurs or scissors are invaluable for a gentle cutting off of the bunches of fruit, otherwise they may fall to the ground before reaching your container; if being gathered from the wild, a porous container is essential for the journey home, in order to avoid the development of mould on the berries; in any case, winemaking should commence without delay after the harvesting. A kitchen fork is best for separating the berries from their stalks.

Elderberries ready for harvesting. ▶

INGREDIENTS

It is advisable to boil all water used for winemaking. It is not unknown for tapwater to contain so much chlorine that one is almost persuaded that the open tap is served from the public swimming baths; and yeast is killed by chlorine.

Having boiled the water, it is then advisable to aerate it by pouring through a funnel into the primary fermentation vessel; this because yeast needs oxygen in order to multiply into an adequate workforce for the fermentation job assigned to it. Stirring of the must (the mixture of basic ingredients and water) during the aerobic fermentation also increases the oxygen content derived from the air, and has the additional practical value of keeping the solids saturated with water in order to release their goodness.

It is recommended that 'soft' water should have a pinch per gallon of magnesium sulphate (Epsom salts) added, in order to ensure that the yeast is enabled to conduct a reasonably rapid fermentation.

Most tapwaters are alkaline, and wine yeast needs an acidic environment in order to thrive; our formulations will therefore include acids which otherwise would not be present in the must in sufficient quantities.

Yeast nutrients and energisers are included, with which to ensure trouble-free, non-sticking fermentations; the quality of the wine produced is unaffected by a surfeit of these ingredients, but a shortage can slow down or even stop a fermentation.

Since nitrogen and phosphate are essential to a good fermentation, this is ensured by the use of ammonium phosphate.

Yeast growth is assisted by an adequate supply of vitamin B_1, which can be purchased as 3 mg. Benerva tablets, or you may have readily to hand a jar of Marmite, when half a teaspoonful per gallon of must will be adequate.

The maximum weight of elderberries used is 1.36 kg. per 4.55 litres (3 lb. per gallon), since otherwise a surfeit of tannin would be evident as a bitter taste in the finished wine, which only long maturation in an oak cask or in a 'wine-five' would alleviate. The tannin is present not only in the skins (where it is to be found in most red-skinned fruits), but also in appreciable quantities in the juice. We need some tannin in all wines, of course, otherwise we'd finish up with an insipid taste lacking the desired astringency and zest. When gathering your elderberries, it is helpful to know that 2.72 kg. (6 lb.) will fill a 4.55 litre (1 gal.) bucket. It can also be of assistance to be aware that 453 g. (1 lb.) of elderberries will yield about 568 ml. (1 pint) of juice, and that 113 g. (¼ lb.) of dried elderberries equals 453 g. (1 lb.) of the fresh fruit. Elderberries are the more readily gathered in their natural bunches, when the berries can be removed from the stalks by the means of a household dinner fork. A wide-toothed new comb may appear to offer advantages over a fork, but the stalks tend to tangle among the teeth of the comb, and it is only too easy to finish up with a shortage of teeth left on the comb.

Elderflowers (white, not cream-coloured) and rosepetals are used to provide a pleasing bouquet to our wines. You may wish to use white rosepetals in white wines (produced with green, ripe elderberries). Gather the elderflowers on a dry, sunny day when they are fully open, and cut them off the stalks with scissors. The elderflowers must be dried if they are to be used with our elderberries, since there is normally a gap of one month between the last of the flowers and the first ripening of the berries. The weights of dried elderflowers required per 4.55 litre (one gallon) of wine are so small as to present weighing-out difficulties, but this problem is not so acute when a 22.73 litre (5 gallon) batch of wine is being made. However, one can overcome the problem by measuring out separate small volumes of the flowers and hanging them up to dry in muslin bags – 425 ml. (¾ pint) batches would be appropriate, their weight being 8 grammes fully dried. Alternatively, it is not too difficult to make a simple balance, and if you don't have any gramme weights, it is sufficient for our purpose to take a one penny coin as weighing 3 grammes. Such a weight of dried flowers is readily separated into (say) three equal piles, each of which will weigh one gramme.

Rosepetals are normally still available when the first elderberries are ripe, and if the blooms have been removed during their season, as required by good husbandry, fresh flowers should be available for the entire season of elderberry gathering. Fresh rosepetals present no difficulty so far as measuring by volume (not pressed down) is concerned.

The flowers are put into a nylon bag, and immersed in the wine must for three days after the first vigorous, frothy fermentation has subsided.

Bananas will be simmered in water for 30 minutes and the juice strained off – do not press out.

Parsnips will be simmered in water only until they are tender, not mushy (about 10 minutes).

Pectozyme is used not only to ensure that bright, sparkling wines without haze are produced, but also to break down the flesh of fruits and secure a better extraction therefrom, thus improving wine quality. Pectozyme is killed by hot water.

It will be noted that the intention is to ferment all our wines to dryness, and thus enable us to produce medium-dry, medium-sweet and sweet wines with a greater degree of precision; this is dealt with under a sub-heading of the Methods described for the production of our wines.

Honey is prepared for use by simmering in its own volume of water for 10 minutes. The sugar content is invert sugar, suitable for our Sparkling Table wines.

Syrup can be prepared by pouring boiling water on to sugar, and stirring to dissolve, using 568 ml. (one pint) of water to 907 g. (2 lb.) of sugar, which gives 1.136 litre (two pints) of syrup; other quantities in proportion.

Invert sugar, for use in Sparkling Table wines is prepared by simmering 907 g. (2 lb.) of household white granulated sugar (sucrose), or the amount given in the recipe, with one teaspoonful of citric acid in 568 ml. (one pint) of water until the syrup is straw-coloured, which indicates that your sugar has then been inverted (about 15 minutes). If you purchase invert sugar, then for every 453 g. (pound) weight of sucrose given in the recipe you will need 570 g. (1¼ lb.) of invert sugar.

Our yeast starter for 4.55 to 13.64 litre (1 to 3 gal.) of must is:

28 g. sugar (1 oz.)
284 ml. water at 24°C (75°F) (10 fl. oz.)
½ tsp. tartaric acid
½ tsp. ammonium phosphate
1 – 3 mg. Benerva tablet
1 tsp. Formula 67 yeast

These amounts are doubled for 13.64 to 27.28 litre of must.

Although a quicker fermentation is attained by higher temperatures, it must be remembered that yeast should never be subjected to a higher temperature than 28°C (82°F), Tokay yeast excepted, since beyond this maximum it is under stress, and will be finally killed off at 40°C (104°F). It should also be kept in mind that the process of fermentation raises the temperature of the must. Never put a fermentation jar in the sun to warm up – ultraviolet rays also kill yeast. At 18°C (66°F) yeast activity begins to slow down, and it ceases at 4°C (40°F). Fluctuations in temperature should also be avoided – do not stand the demijohn in a draught.

EQUIPMENT

Much of the equipment required for the labour-saving wine-making described herein will be found amongst your kitchen utensils. All the recipes given are for 4.55 litre (one gallon) batches of wine, but of course multiples of this basic measure are then readily practicable.

Our first requirement is that all the utensils and equipment to be used in each and every winemaking operation shall be sterilised, and that this shall be executed just before they come into contact with any ingredient which we are using. For this we need:

Weighing-out scales
Measuring jug
White plastic long-handled spoon
White plastic bucket, minimum 2.27 litre (½ gal.) capacity
White plastic bucket for drip-drying small items
Screw-stoppered litre or quart bottle

The first actual winemaking operation to be tackled is that of the preparation of a yeast starter. For this we require:

Wide-mouthed 568 ml. (pint) bottle
Cottonwool plug for bottle
Saucepan with lid
White plastic 12.5 cm. (5 in.) diameter funnel
Source of heat to maintain 24°C (75°F)
(Cylinder cupboard or preferably electric heater tray)

When a Sparkling Table wine is being made, and if invert sugar is not readily available, then white granulated household sugar (sucrose) should be inverted, since we will need to detect any remaining fermentable sugar in our wine at the apparent conclusion (as shown by a hydrometer reading of less than 1.000) of the fermentation process, and sucrose is not readily detectable in small quantities, whereas sugar testing kits will expose very small amounts of invert sugar. The hydrometer will measure larger amounts of sucrose, of course, but will not differentiate between sucrose and other suspended matter in solution, of which there is normally a small amount. All this is very important, since too much fermentable sugar in the finished wine can lead to burst bottles, or at the least uncontrollable frothing and loss of wine when pouring. It cannot be stressed too often that champagne bottles which have been carefully examined for a lack of flaws are essential for sparkling wines. To prepare invert sugar we need:

Weighing-out scales
Enamel or non-stick saucepan with lid
White plastic long-handled spoon

A metal saucepan, with which the acid used in this process can react to produce off-flavours, must not be used. An unchipped enamel finish is satisfactory.

The next process is the treatment of the water required for our winemaking, for which we require:

Kettle or saucepan with lid
White plastic funnel

By these means the water can be cleared of chlorine and then aerated by pouring through the funnel, when cool, on to the main ingredients. Soft water should have a pinch of magnesium sulphate (Epsom salts) added at the same time.

We are now ready to get the main business of winemaking under way, for which we need:

Can opener
Plastic potato masher
Weighing-out scales
Saucepan, 4 litre (7 pint)
Bucket, white plastic, 9.1 litre (2 gal.), Two
Butter muslin, sheet 61 cm. (2 ft.) square, Two
Long-handled white plastic spoon
Nylon filter bag
White plastic funnel, 22.5 cm. (9 in.) diameter
Fermentation jar (demijohn), 4.55 litre (1 gal.)
Plastic bowl for jar
Fermentation lock and bored rubber bung
Clear plastic tube 6 mm. bore (¼ in.), 1.8 m. long (6 ft.)
Hydrometer
Measuring cylinder (hydrometer jar)
Immersion thermometer and air thermometer
Filter bag, canvas
Glass U-bend for plastic tube, and tap
Cylinder cupboard or electric heater tray set at 24°C (75°F) for
    red wines and at 21°C (70°F) for white wines
Wine filtering apparatus
6 winebottles
6 corks and capsules
Mallet
Corking tool
15 cm. (6 in.) length thin strong string
6 winebottle labels

If red wines are to retain their colour, they must be protected from light. Personally, I do not like coloured demijohns because it is not easy to examine their contents, and a sheet of brown paper wrapped around the jar and held in position with an elastic band is quite satisfactory. Coloured bottles are, of course, essential for red wines.

For storage and serving we require:
Winebottle rack and a dry room at 13°C (55°F)
Corkscrew
Decanter
Tulip-shaped clear wineglasses

It is worth repeating that still white wines benefit considerably by transference to the decanter an hour before drinking; red wines preferably longer – up to half a day for red dessert wines.

For Sparkling Table wines we also need:
6 champagne bottles
7 plastic champagne bottle stoppers
Punch to fit over dome of stoppers
Mallet
24 gauge mild steel wire for 12 bottles, 4.6 m. (15 ft.) long
Wire cutters – pliers
Plastic bucket
Gloves for handling bottles from deep-freeze
Small plastic spoon, or saltspoon, or mint sauce spoon
Or, in lieu of the above-given items:
Sparklets syphon and carbon dioxide gas cylinders
For winemaking in bulk we require:
9.1 litre (2 gal.) plastic barrel and/or
22.7 litre (5 gal.) plastic barrel
Jumbo fermentation locks and bored corks to fit barrels
22.7 litre (5 gal.) white plastic container with lid
Butter muslin to overlap top of container by 30 cm. (12 in.) all round
Large size white plastic funnel

The winemaker will probably confine himself (herself) to the production of Table wines in bulk, and since these wines are also imbibed in quantity, and regularly, it saves labour to bottle in a 2 and a 2.5 litre bottle per 4.55 litre (gallon) of wine.

The use of certain items of winemaking equipment may need some clarification:

An immersion thermometer will only give a true reading when the column of mercury is completely submerged – this means that after immersion of the thermometer it is gradually lowered into the liquor until the rising column of mercury no longer shows above the surface.

The hydrometer must be read with the eye at the level of the top of the column of liquid, when the true level will be found to be lower (and the reading higher) than is apparent at first glance, because the liquid creeps up the glass due to surface tension. Since we are producing dry wines, to be sweetened (if so desired) after fermentation is complete, we will be fermenting onwards until a hydrometer reading of less than 1.000 is attained, when fermentation will finally have ceased, and the future risk of bursting bottles will have been eliminated so far as is reasonably practicable. Non-fermentable saccharin pellets will be used to produce medium-dry, medium-sweet, and sweet wines.

In the case of Sparkling Table wines, we will require to check that all the sugar has completely fermented out when the hydrometer indicates that this is so – we will not be using Campden tablets in these wines at this stage. This essential task (to avoid the risk of bursting bottles due to excess carbon dioxide gas being produced by the secondary fermentation in the bottle) is effected either by means of the Clinitest (available at chemists – produced for the use of diabetics), or by a proprietary testing kit obtainable from home-winemaking shops. These kits come with full instructions for their use, which need not, therefore, be discussed herein.

Siphoning or racking is the process of transferring a liquor from a vessel in which the debris of ingredients and/or of yeast has deposited on the bottom, into a clean vessel. It is effected by lowering a glass U-tube on the end of plastic tubing to the bottom of the vessel to be emptied, which is stood on a worktop, and taking a quick intake of breath on the other end of the tube to start the syphon, when it is immediately dropped into the receiving vessel, which is stood on the floor in a bowl. White wines require that the end of the tube rests on the bottom of the receiving vessel, so that it is not aerated (oxygen can spoil the colour and taste of the finished wine). Red Dessert wines are a special case – they can be aerated by the discharge end of the tube resting near the top of the receiving vessel.

A small but important point to remember when bottling wine is that a piece of thin strong string must be looped over the neck of the bottle to reach below driven cork level, leaving sufficient string outside to grasp for its withdrawal when the cork has been driven home. This is to release the air in the bottle which otherwise would be under pressure and tend to blow out the cork.

A champagne bottle stopper is wired down by means of a 40 cm. (15 in.) long wire looped 2 cm. (¾ in.) diameter from the centre and twisted 3 cm. (1 in.) long, the free ends passed round the lower flange on the bottle and twisted to near the top of the stopper 3 cm. (1 in.) long, then one end is passed through the first-mentioned loop sited at the directly opposite side of the bottle neck, and twisted on the other end to bring the loop over the dome of the stopper.

It is helpful to have containers marked for capacity; this is usually marked on the inside of the vessel when done commercially. Plastic containers without such markings are normally translucent and can be marked on the outside in indelible ink or by any other means favoured by the winemaker.

A log book is an essential item of equipment for the winemaker, and should not be overlooked. The more meticulously it is entered up, the more readily will you be able to reproduce favourite wines, and even be able to pinpoint the very occasional time when a slip-up has been made – we do all make mistakes at varying intervals.

STERILIZATION

Sulphur dioxide gas is our defence against harmful bacteria, and is obtained from Campden tablets or from sodium metabisulphite powder. Warm water (not hot) is used in which to dissolve these substances, otherwise the gas given off would be lost before it could do its job, and the user would need to stand well clear of the choking fumes – normally, the gas is hardly noticeable.

All equipment should be rinsed in a solution of sodium metabisulphite immediately before use, and with particular reference to buckets, demijohns, corks and bottles. It will be remembered that we are using a sterilising agent, and that visual cleansing (with the aid of Chempro SDP or the like, if necessary) will already have been carried out. For this purpose, dissolve 113 g. (¼ lb.) of sodium metabisulphite in 1.14 litre (¼ gal.) of water, and after dealing with the buckets and demijohn etc., store in a tightly screw-stoppered litre or quart lemonade or suchlike clean bottle until required for the corks and winebottles; it should still be evident by smell that sulphur dioxide gas is being given off, even after the maximum of four months storage.

It is the more convenient to use Campden tablets for the musts and the embryo wines. Two Campden tablets per 4.55 litre (gallon) of must is adequate. The yeast must not be added until 24 hours later. At the final racking, particularly for white wines, one Campden tablet per 4.55 litre (gallon) is added; in the case of white wines, this is to reduce oxidation, and the second purpose is to ensure that no active yeast remains in any wine which is ready for storage. This final racking procedure does not, however, apply to Sparkling Table wines.

Honey must be simmered for ten minutes in at the least its own volume of water (to reduce frothing trouble) in order to render it sterile.

Fresh bananas will be simmered for thirty minutes, and the extracted juice will thus be sterile. Fresh parsnips will be simmered only until tender (about ten minutes) and will then also be sterile.

THE SIX METHODS

METHOD A

APERITIF – TABLE – SOCIAL WINES

Elderberries

1st Day – Sprinkle the elderberries into a container in thin layers, crushing each succeeding layer with a potato masher. Just cover with boiled water cooled to room temperature, add two Campden tablets, cover, and leave for two days.

2nd Day – Prepare the yeast starter.

3rd Day – Add the yeast starter, together with the sugar or honey syrup, acids, Benerva tablet, ammonium phosphate, nutrient and energiser to the elderberries, together with boiled, cooled and aerated water to reach the 4.55 litre (one-gallon) mark, and keep covered at 24°C (75°F).

4th Day – Place the crushed or finely cut up other fruit into another container, together with the juice from the can, add cool boiled water if necessary to just cover the fruit, add two Campden tablets plus any Pectozyme given in the recipe, and leave for one day.

5th Day – Strain the elderberries off the juice, press out, set aside for re-use in another wine, and pour the liquor into a container, adding the fruit pulp and juice from the other fruit; keep covered at 24°C (75°F).

8th Day – Add the flower petals contained in a filter bag.

11th Day – Take out the flower petals, and strain the liquor into a demijohn and on to the banana syrup (if any in recipe) and grape concentrate; top up with warm water, fit holed bung and part water-filled fermentation lock; maintain the temperature at 24°C (75°F).

15th Day – If the passage of bubbles through the fermentation lock appears to have stopped, take a hydrometer reading; if this is less than 1.000 take readings at three-day intervals until identical readings are obtained – probably at 0.993. The Table wines can take up to ten days longer to reach this stage; the Aperitif and Social wines will take a little longer than the Table wines – the maintenance of the correct temperature of the must influences the speed of the fermentation. When the steady low reading on the hydrometer is attained, syphon off from the yeast deposit, add one Campden tablet, top up with warm water, refit the holed bung and part water-filled fermentation lock, and store for one month, preferably at 13°C (55°F).

The wine can then be bottled, but it will gain a more attractive crystal clearness if it is filtered before bottling. The filtering apparatus comes with full instructions for its use.

METHOD B

APERITIF – TABLE – SOCIAL WINES

Elderflowers

1st Day – Prepare the yeast starter. Place the crushed or finely cut up fruit into a container, together with the juice from the can, add cooled boiled water if necessary to just cover the fruit, add two Campden tablets plus any Pectozyme given in the recipe.

2nd Day – Add the yeast starter, together with the sugar or honey syrup, acids, Benerva tablet, ammonium phosphate, nutrient and energiser to the fruit pulp and juice, together with boiled, cooled and aerated water to reach the 4.55 litre (one gallon) mark, and keep covered at 21°C (70°F).

7th Day – Add the flower petals contained in a filter bag.

10th Day – Take out the flower petals, and strain the liquor into a demijohn and on to the banana syrup (if in the recipe) and the grape concentrate; top up with warm water, fit holed bung and part water-filled fermentation lock; maintain the temperature at 21°C (70°F).

14th Day – Proceed as for the 15th day of elderberries, Method A.

METHOD C

DESSERT WINES

Elderberries

1st Day – Sprinkle the elderberries into a container in thin layers, crushing each succeeding layer with a potato masher. Just cover with boiled water cooled to room temperature, add two Campden tablets, cover, and leave for two days.

2nd Day – Prepare the yeast starter.

3rd Day – Add the yeast starter, together with the sugar or honey syrup, acids, Benerva tablet, ammonium phosphate, nutrient and energiser to the elderberries, together with boiled, cooled and aerated water to reach the 4.55 litre (one gallon) mark, and keep covered at 24°C (75°F).

4th Day – Place the crushed or finely cut up other fruit into another container together with the juice from the can, add cooled boiled water if necessary to just cover the fruit, add two Campden tablets plus any Pectozyme given in the recipe, and leave for one day.

5th Day – Strain the elderberries off the juice, press out, set aside for re-use in another wine, and pour the liquor into a container, adding the fruit pulp and juice from the other fruit; keep covered at 24°C (75°F).

8th Day – Add the flower petals contained in a filter bag.

11th Day – Take out the flower petals, and strain the liquor into a demijohn and on to the banana syrup (if in recipe) and half of the given amount of grape concentrate, top up if necessary, but so as to leave room for the other half of grape concentrate, which will be added later in two equal amounts. Fit holed bung and part water-filled fermentation lock; maintain the temperature at 24°C (75°F).

17th Day – Take a hydrometer reading, and if the fermentation is down to 1.010 add half the remaining grape concentrate.

23rd Day – Take a hydrometer reading, and if the fermentation is again down to 1.010 add the remaining grape concentrate.

30th Day – If the passage of bubbles through the fermentation lock appears to have stopped, take a hydrometer reading; if this is less than 1.000, take readings at three-day intervals until identical readings are obtained – probably at 0.994. The maintenance of the correct temperature of the must has a considerable influence on the speed of the fermentation. When the steady low reading on the hydrometer is attained, syphon off from the yeast deposit, add one Campden tablet, top up with warm water, refit the holed bung and part water-filled fermentation lock, and store for one month, preferably at 13°C (55°F).

The wine can now be bottled, but it will gain a more attractive crystal clearness if it is filtered before bottling. The filtering apparatus comes with full instructions for its use.

METHOD D

SPARKLING TABLE WINES

Elderberries

1st Day – Sprinkle the elderberries into a container in thin layers, crushing each succeeding layer with a potato masher. Just cover with boiled water cooled to room temperature, add two Campden tablets, cover, and leave for two days.

2nd Day – Prepare the yeast starter.

3rd Day – Add the yeast starter, together with the inverted sugar or the honey syrup, acids, Benerva tablet, ammonium phosphate, nutrient and energiser to the elderberries, together with boiled, cooled and aerated water to reach the 3.4 litre (¾ gal.) mark, and keep covered at 24°C (75°F).

4th Day – Place the crushed or finely cut up other fruit into another container, together with the juice from the can, add cool boiled water if necessary to just cover the fruit, add two Campden tablets plus any Pectozyme given in the recipe, and leave for one day.

5th Day – Strain the elderberries off the juice, press out, set aside for re-use in another wine, and pour the liquor into a container, adding the fruit pulp and juice from the other fruit; keep covered at 24°C (75°F).

8th Day – Add the flower petals contained in a filter bag.

11th Day – Take out the flower petals, and strain the liquor into a demijohn and on to the banana syrup (if in recipe) and the grape concentrate; top up with warm water, fit holed bung and part water-filled fermentation lock; maintain the temperature at 24°C (75°F).

15th Day – If the passage of bubbles through the fermentation lock appears to have stopped, take a hydrometer reading; if this is less than 1.000 take readings at three-day intervals until identical readings are obtained – probably at 0.990. The maintenance of the correct temperature of the must influences the speed of the fermentation. When the steady low reading on the hydrometer is attained, we have alternative modes of procedure open to us; one of these will result in a better quality wine than the other which will be described, but demands considerable patience in its execution, and the expertise necessary to carry it to fruition may not be immediately forthcoming. We will therefore proceed to the eighteenth day to describe a trouble-free, 'quickie' method of imparting sparkle to our wine, and after that we will return to the eighteenth day of our alternative method (18th Day (a) and 18th Day (b)).

18th Day (a) – Siphon the liquor off from the yeast deposit, add one Campden tablet, top up with warm water, refit the holed bung and part water-filled fermentation lock, and store for one month, preferably at 13°C (55°F).

Now filter the wine, after which, pour sufficient of it to fill a carbonating siphon bottle, screw on the top, and insert an 8 gm. carbon dioxide cartridge to admit the whole of its gas. Press trigger with the siphon bottle upside down, and when the escape of gas ceases turn the bottle the right way up again. Remove the top, pour out into glasses, and drink the rest in the bottle without undue delay. The colder the wine, the longer it will retain the sparkle thus imparted. The rest of the 4.55 litre (gallon) of wine should be bottled and stored in the usual way, ready for the next time it is desired to impart this type of sparkle to it.

18th Day (b) – The wine must now be tested for residual sugar. This is very important if the dangerous bursting of bottles is to be avoided. The test is carried out with a Clinitest outfit (sold at chemists for the use of diabetics) or with a sugar-testing outfit obtainable from home-winemaking shops complete with full instructions. The maximum acceptable sugar content is 1%. If one of these tests indicates a greater amount, the wine must either be left to see if the fermentation will continue, or be blended with another wine of considerably less than 1% sugar content, in order to achieve this figure, or be imbibed as a still wine. It is not worthwhile to treat it as a 'stuck' fermentation when this stage has been reached. This problem will arise only when a mistake has been made somewhere along the line.

The wine is then filtered.

The champagne bottles (no others are to be used) must be absolutely clean internally (to allow the sediment free movement over the glass at a later stage), and perfect – entirely free from flaws in the glass.

It is also essential that excessive pressure should not be introduced by the gas evolved in the secondary fermentation, as would result from too much sugar in the bottles. These are the maximum amounts of a stock sugar solution, per bottle, for use with the results of the sugar test:

$$
\begin{aligned}
0.0\% &= 14 \text{ ml.} \\
0.25\% &= 13 \text{ ml.} \\
0.5\% &= 12 \text{ ml.} \\
0.75\% &= 7 \text{ ml.} \\
1.0\% &= 6 \text{ ml.}
\end{aligned}
$$

A 5 ml. (cc) teaspoon (provided with some medicines) may be used to give the smaller measures required. The reading of the measuring cylinder (hydrometer jar) must be made with the eye at the level of the surface of the liquid. The stock sugar solution is made up by bringing briefly to the boil 226 g. (½ lb.) sugar in 142 ml. (¼ pint) water, giving 284 ml. (½ pint) of sugar solution.

You will need another 168 ml. (6 fl. oz.) of this sugar syrup when the degorgement takes place. Having prepared the bottles and allowed the sugar solution to cool to room temperature in another sterile bottle, the wine is funnelled into the champagne bottles to within 8 cm. (3 in.) of the top, followed by the carefully measured sugar syrup, after which the bottles are stoppered to await the yeast starter. Prepare this all in accordance with the yeast starter described earlier, but using champagne yeast, bearing in mind that 7 ml. will be required for each of six bottles, i.e., 42 ml. or 1½ fl. oz. After 24 hours, or when the starter is in vigorous action, add the required amount to each bottle, which should now be full to within 5 cm. (2 in.), and not less than 4 cm. (1½ in.) of the top; check this measurement, since the space left available affects the pressure in the bottle. The plastic champagne stoppers should now be made pliable in warm water, and fitted to the bottles with the aid of a punch fitting tool (hollowed to fit over the dome of the stopper) and mallet, followed by wiring down. The bottles are then upended a few times to mix the yeast starter and the sugar syrup, and kept at about 19°C (65°F) for the secondary fermentation, stored in a winerack (i.e., in a horizontal position). The tightening of the wiring, due to the stopper tending to push out a little, indicates that all is going well with the production of carbon dioxide gas.

After three months, a yeast deposit will be apparent on the underside of the bottles, and they should now be stored upside-down at about 13°C (55°F); during this time, the bottles should be gently agitated, firstly to prevent the yeast deposit sticking to the side of the bottles, and secondly to assist it to settle in the stopper.

After another three months, or after nine months if you are prepared to wait for a better quality wine, place the bottles, still stopper downwards, in a deep freezer until ice is visible just beyond the stopper (may be about half-an-hour) – do not leave until the ice extends too far beyond this point, or the yeast may be difficult to remove. In the meantime, prepare 168 ml. (6 fl. oz.) sugar syrup, all as last described, and put it in the freezer for the final ten minutes with the wine. The garage, or a shed is the best place to execute the degorgement now required – just in case of accidents to the wine – your freezer may be there in any case. Hold the winebottle pointing slightly downwards into a bucket (a bottle angle bracket can be bought for this job), cut off the wire and encourage the frozen yeast to pop out by fiddling with the stopper. A clean stopper can be used to prevent too much wine escaping, if necessary, and then a small plastic spoon can be used to remove any remaining yeast-ice, after which 28 ml. (1 fl. oz.) of the sugar syrup is added, and finally the clean stopper is inserted and wired down (described under Equipment) as before. If a dry wine is preferred, then a still wine can be used instead of the sugar syrup for the topping-up, just described, following the degorgement.

METHOD E

SPARKLING TABLE WINE

Elderflowers

1st Day – Prepare the yeast starter. Place the crushed or finely cut up fruit into a container, together with the juice from the can, add cool boiled water if necessary to just cover the fruit, add two Campden tablets plus any Pectozyme given in the recipe.

2nd Day – Add the yeast starter, together with the inverted sugar or the honey syrup, acids, Benerva tablet, ammonium phosphate, nutrient and energiser to the fruit pulp and juice, together with boiled, cooled and aerated water to reach the 4.55 litre (one gallon) mark, and keep covered at 21°C (70°F).

7th Day – Add the flower petals contained in a filter bag.

10th Day – Take out the flower petals, and strain the liquor into a demijohn on to the grape concentrate; top up with warm water, fit holed bung and part water-filled fermentation lock; maintain the temperature at 21°C (70°F).

14th Day – Proceed as for 15th day of elderberries.

METHOD F

MEDIUM-DRY, MEDIUM-SWEET & SWEET WINES

Elderberry or Elderflower

All our wines have been produced as dry wines, so that the risk of fermentation in still winebottles has been reduced to a negligible minimum, and should be non-existent. Sweeter wines are very easily made from our dry wines by the introduction of non-fermentable saccharin (Sweetex) into the decanter before the wine is poured into it. The suggested amounts, per bottle, are given hereunder. The sweetening has been given as per bottle so that personal taste can modify the figures, if desired, then following such trials six times the given amounts can be added per 4.55 litre (gallon) at the final racking, dissolved in the topping-up water. The sweetening of Sparkling Table wines has been described earlier, to give a dry or a medium-sweet wine.

	Medium-dry	Medium-sweet	Sweet
Aperitif	½	3	6
Table	½	2	5
Dessert	2	5	8
Social	1	4	7

WINE RECIPES

APERITIF

(1)

Ingredients:
284 ml. white (not cream) elderflowers (½ pint)
or 6 g. dried elderflowers
142 ml. rosepetals (¼ pint)
or 1 g. dried rosepetals
994 ml. white grape concentrate (35 fl. oz.)
453 g. sugar (1 lb.)
½ tsp. citric acid
1½ tsp. malic acid
1 tsp. tartaric acid
1 – 3 mg. Benerva tablet
½ tsp. tannin
1 tablet yeast nutrient
½ tsp. ammonium phosphate
½ tsp. yeast energiser
yeast starter
water to 4.55 litre (1 gal.)

Method:
1st Day – Prepare the yeast starter.
2nd Day – Place the grape concentrate and sugar syrup, together with the rest of the ingredients (except the flowers), into a container, fill to the 4.55 litre (1 gal.) mark with boiled, cooled and aerated water, cover, and keep at 21°C (70°F).
7th Day – Add the flowers contained in a filter bag.
10th Day – Take out the flowers, funnel the liquor into a demijohn, top up with warm water if necessary, fit holed bung and part water-filled fermentation lock, and keep at 21°C (70°F).
15th Day – Proceed as for Method A.

(2)

Ingredients:
  907 g. elderberries (2 lb.)
  710 ml. red grape concentrate (25 fl. oz.)
  570 g. sugar (1¼ lb.)
  6 g. dried elderflowers
  or 284 ml. elderflowers (½ pint)
  1 tsp. malic acid
  1 tsp. tartaric acid
  1 – 3 mg. Benerva tablet
  1 tablet yeast nutrient
  ½ tsp. ammonium phosphate
  ½ tsp. yeast energiser
  yeast starter
  water to 4.55 litre (1 gal.)
Method:
  As for Method A, but ignore all mention of 'other fruit'.

(3)

Ingredients:
  907 g. green (ripe) elderberries (2 lb.)
  795 ml. white grape concentrate (28 fl. oz.)
  570 g. sugar (1¼ lb.)
  284 ml. rosepetals (½ pint)
  1 tsp. malic acid
  1 tsp. tartaric acid
  1 – 3 mg. Benerva tablet
  ¼ tsp. tannin
  1 tablet yeast nutrient
  ½ tsp. ammonium phosphate
  ½ tsp. yeast energiser
  yeast starter
  water to 4.55 litre (1 gal.)
Method:
  Method A, ignoring all mention of 'other fruit', and add the tannin at the same time as the yeast starter.

(4)

Ingredients:
   907 g. green (ripe) elderberries (2 lb.)
   568 ml. apple juice, unsweetened (1 pint)
   568 ml. white grape concentrate (1 pint)
   680 g. sugar (1½ lb.)
   284 ml. rosepetals (½ pint)
   1 tsp. malic acid   ½ tsp. ammonium phosphate
   1 tsp. tartaric acid   ½ tsp. yeast energiser
   1 – 3 mg. Benerva tablet   yeast starter
   ¼ tsp. tannin   water to 4.55 litre (1 gal.)
   1 tablet yeast nutrient   2 tsp. Pectozyme
Method:
   Method A, ignoring all mention of 'other fruit', add tannin at the same time as the yeast starter, and add the apple juice with the grape concentrate, together with the Pectozyme.

(5)

Ingredients:
   907 g. green (ripe) elderberries (2 lb.)
   1.14 litre apple juice, unsweetened (1 quart)
   284 ml. white grape concentrate (½ pint)
   907 g. sugar (2 lb.)
   3 g. dried elderflowers
   or 142 ml. elderflowers (¼ pint)
   142 ml. rosepetals (¼ pint)
   1 tsp. malic acid   ½ tsp. ammonium phosphate
   1 tsp. tartaric acid   ½ tsp. yeast energiser
   1 – 3 mg. Benerva tablet   yeast starter
   ¼ tsp. tannin   water to 4.55 litre (1 gal.)
   1 tablet yeast nutrient   4 tsp. Pectozyme
Method:
   Method A, ignoring all mention of 'other fruit', add tannin at the same time as the yeast starter, and add the apple juice with the grape concentrate together with the Pectozyme.

(6)

Ingredients:
  907 g. elderberries (2 lb.)
  568 ml. apple juice, unsweetened (1 pint)
  568 ml. orange juice, unsweetened (1 pint)
  142 ml. white grape concentrate (¼ pint)
  1.02 kg. sugar (2¼ lb.)
  284 ml. rosepetals (½ pint)
  ½ tsp. malic acid
  ½ tsp. tartaric acid   ½ tsp. yeast energiser
  1 – 3 mg. Benerva tablet   yeast starter
  1 tablet yeast nutrient   water to 4.55 litre (1 gal.)
  ½ tsp. ammonium phosphate   2 tsp. Pectozyme
Method:
  Method A, ignoring all mention of 'other fruit', adding the apple and orange juices with the grape concentrate, together with the Pectozyme.

(7)

Ingredients:
  907 g. green (ripe) elderberries (2 lb.)
  907 g. apricots, canned (2 lb.)
  568 ml. white grape concentrate (1 pint)
  680 g. sugar (1½ lb.)
  6 g. dried elderflowers
  or 284 ml. elderflowers (½ pint)
  1 tsp. malic acid
  1 tsp. tartaric acid
  1 – 3 mg. Benerva tablet
  ¼ tsp. tannin
  1 tablet yeast nutrient   yeast starter
  ½ tsp. ammonium phosphate   water to 4.55 litre (1 gal.)
  ½ tsp. yeast energiser   2 tsp. Pectozyme
Method:
  All as Method A

(8)

Ingredients:
907 g. elderberries (2 lb.)
1.82 kg. apricots, canned (4 lb.)
284 ml. white grape concentrate (½ pint)
795 g. sugar (1¾ lb.)
284 ml. rosepetals (½ pint)
1 tsp. malic acid
1 tsp. tartaric acid   ½ tsp. yeast energiser
1 – 3 mg. Benerva tablet   yeast starter
1 tablet yeast nutrient   water to 4.55 litre (1 gal.)
½ tsp. ammonium phosphate   4 tsp. Pectozyme
Method:
All as Method A.

(9)

Ingredients:
907 g. elderberries (2 lb.)
907 g. beetroot (2 lb.)
1.36 kg. apricots, canned (3 lb.)
284 ml. red grape concentrate (½ pint)
795 g. sugar (1¾ lb.)
3 g. dried elderflowers
or 142 ml. elderflowers (¼ pint)
142 ml. rosepetals (¼ pint)
1½ tsp. malic acid
1 tsp. tartaric acid
1 – 3 mg. Benerva tablet
1 tablet yeast nutrient
½ tsp. ammonium phosphate
½ tsp. yeast energiser
yeast starter
water to 4.55 litre (1 gal.)
3 tsp. Pectozyme
Method:
Method A, adding the beetroot liquor on the 11th day – the
beetroot must be exceptionally well scrubbed but not peeled, then

diced into a saucepan, just covered with water, and simmered until just tender and not mushy (from one to two hours according to size – the skins will rub off with your finger when ready), after which it is strained off the liquor.

(10)

Ingredients:
 907 g. green (ripe) elderberries (2 lb.)
 1.82 kg. gooseberries, canned (4 lb.)
 453 g. bananas (1 lb.)
 284 ml. white grape concentrate (½ pint)   ¼ tsp. tannin
 907 g. honey (2 lb.)   1 tablet yeast nutrient
 6 g. dried elderflowers   ½ tsp. ammonium phosphate
 or 284 ml. elderflowers (½ pint) ½ tsp. yeast energiser
 1 tsp. malic acid   yeast starter
 1 tsp. tartaric acid   water to 4.55 litre (1 gal.)
 1 – 3 mg. Benerva tablet   4 tsp. Pectozyme

Method:
 Method A, not forgetting the drill for the preparation of the honey and banana syrups.

(11)

Ingredients:
 907 g. elderberries (2 lb.)
 907 g. greengages, canned (2 lb.)
 284 ml. white grape concentrate (½ pint)
 907 g. sugar (2 lb.)
 6 g. dried elderflowers
 or 284 ml. elderflowers (½ pint)
 1 tsp. malic acid
 1 tsp. tartaric acid   ½ tsp. yeast energiser
 1 – 3 mg. Benerva tablet   yeast starter
 1 tablet yeast nutrient   water to 4.55 litre (1 gal.)
 ½ tsp. ammonium phosphate   2 tsp. Pectozyme

Method:
 Method A

(12)

Ingredients:
   907 g. elderberries (2 lb.)
   568 ml. orange juice, unsweetened (1 pint)
   568 ml. red grape concentrate (1 pint)
   680 g. sugar (1½ lb.)
   284 ml. rosepetals (½ pint)
   or 2 g. dried rosepetals
   1 tsp. malic acid
   1 tsp. tartaric acid
   1 – 3 mg. Benerva tablet
   1 tablet yeast nutrient
   ½ tsp. ammonium phosphate
   ½ tsp. yeast energiser
   yeast starter
   water to 4.55 litre (1 gal.)
Method:
   Method A, ignoring all mention of 'other fruit', and adding the
orange juice with the grape concentrate.

(13)

Ingredients:
   907 g. green (ripe) elderberries (2 lb.)
   1.14 litre orange juice, unsweetened (1 quart)
   284 ml. white grape concentrate (½ pint)
   907 g. sugar (2 lb.)
   6 g. dried elderflowers
   or 284 ml. elderflowers (½ pint)
   ½ tsp. malic acid
   ½ tsp. tartaric acid   ½ tsp. ammonium phosphate
   1 – 3 mg. Benerva tablet   ½ tsp. yeast energiser
   ¼ tsp. tannin   yeast starter
   1 tablet yeast nutrient   water to 4.55 litre (1 gal.)
Method:
   Method A, ignoring all mention of 'other fruit', and adding the
orange juice with the grape concentrate.

(14)

Ingredients:
  907 g. elderberries (2 lb.)
  568 ml. orange juice, unsweetened (1 pint)
  453 g. peaches, canned (1 lb.)
  284 ml. white grape concentrate (½ pint)
  907 g. sugar (2 lb.)
  284 ml. rosepetals (½ pint)
  or 2 g. dried rosepetals
  ½ tsp. malic acid
  ½ tsp. tartaric acid
  1 – 3 mg. Benerva tablet
  1 tablet yeast nutrient
  ½ tsp. ammonium phosphate
  ½ tsp. yeast energiser
  yeast starter
  water to 4.55 litre (1 gal.)
  1 tsp. Pectozyme
Method:
  Method A and add the orange juice with the grape concentrate.

(15)

Ingredients:
  907 g. elderberries (2 lb.)
  907 g. parsnips (2 lb.)
  568 ml. white grape concentrate (1 pint)
  453 g. bananas (1 lb.)
  680 g. sugar (1½ lb.)
  6 g. dried elderflowers
  or 284 ml. elderflowers (½ pint)
  1 tsp. malic acid
  1 tsp. tartaric acid
  1 – 3 mg. Benerva tablet
  1 tablet yeast nutrient   yeast starter
  ½ tsp. ammonium phosphate   water to 4.55 litre (1 gal.)
  ½ tsp. yeast energiser   2 tsp. Pectozyme

Method:
Method A, but for 'other fruit' read parsnip liquor – made by meticulously scrubbing the frosted parsnips absolutely clean, simmering the sliced pieces until tender, not mushy, (about 10 minutes), and straining them off the liquor. The production of banana syrup has been described. The Pectozyme is required for the parsnips, all as described for 'other fruit' in the standard method.

(16)

Ingredients:
907 g. green (ripe) elderberries (2 lb.)   W
1.36 kg. peaches, canned (3 lb.)
453 g. bananas (1 lb.)
284 ml. white grape concentrate (½ pint)
795 g. sugar (1¾ lb.)
284 ml. rosepetals (½ pint)
or 2 g. dried rosepetals
1 tsp. malic acid
1 tsp. tartaric acid
1 – 3 mg. Benerva tablet
¼ tsp. tannin
1 tablet yeast nutrient
½ tsp. ammonium phosphate
½ tsp. yeast energiser
yeast starter
water to 4.55 litre (1 gal.)
3 tsp. Pectozyme

Method:
Method A, not forgetting the production of the banana syrup.

(17)

Ingredients:
907 g. green (ripe) elderberries (2 lb.)
907 g. pears, canned (2 lb.)
568 ml. white grape concentrate (1 pint)
570 g. sugar (1¼ lb.)
6 g. dried elderflowers
or 284 ml. elderflowers
1 tsp. malic acid
1 tsp. tartaric acid
1 – 3 mg. Benerva tablet
¼ tsp. tannin
1 tablet yeast nutrient
½ tsp. ammonium phosphate
½ tsp. yeast energiser
yeast starter
water to 4.55 litre (1 gal.)
Method:
Method A.

(18)

Ingredients:
907 g. elderberries (2 lb.)
341 ml. rosehip syrup (12 fl. oz. bottle)
284 ml. white grape concentrate (½ pint)
680 g. sugar (1½ lb.)
284 ml. rosepetals (½ pint)
or 2 g. dried rosepetals
1 tsp. malic acid
1 tsp. tartaric acid
1 – 3 mg Benerva tablet
1 tablet yeast nutrient
½ tsp. ammonium phosphate   yeast starter
½ tsp. yeast energiser   water to 4.55 litre (1 gal.)
Method:
Method A, ignoring all mention of 'other fruit' and adding the rosehip syrup with the grape concentrate.

TABLE WINES

(19)

Ingredients:

284 ml. elderflowers (½ pint) (white, not cream-coloured)
852 ml. white grape concentrate (1½ pint)
226 g. sugar (½ lb.)
½ tsp. citric acid
1 tsp. malic acid
½ tsp. tartaric acid
1 – 3 mg. Benerva tablet
1 tablet yeast nutrient
½ tsp. ammonium phosphate
½ tsp. yeast energiser
yeast starter
water to 4.55 litre (1 gal.)

Method:

1st Day – Prepare the yeast starter.

2nd Day – Place the grape concentrate and sugar syrup, together with the yeast starter and the rest of the ingredients (except the flowers) into a container, fill to the 4.55 litre (1 gal.) mark with boiled, cooled and aerated water, cover, and keep at 21°C (70°F).

7th Day – Add the flowers contained in a filter bag.

10th Day – Take out the flowers, funnel the liquor into a demijohn, top up with warm water if necessary, fit holed bung and part water-filled fermentation lock, and keep at 21°C (70°F).

15th Day – Proceed as for Method A.

(20)

Ingredients:
   680 g. elderberries (1½ lb.)   R
   454 ml. red grape concentrate (16 fl. oz.)
   453 g. sugar (1 lb.)
   4 g. dried elderflowers
   or 213 ml. elderflowers (7½ fl. oz.)
   1 tsp. malic acid
   ½ tsp. tartaric acid
   1 – 3 mg. Benerva tablet
   1 tablet yeast nutrient
   ½ tsp. ammonium phosphate
   ½ tsp. yeast energiser
   yeast starter
   water to 4.55 litre (1 gal.)
Method:
Method A, but ignore all mention of 'other fruit'.

(21)

Ingredients:
   680 g. green (ripe) elderberries (1½ lb.)   W
   454 ml. white grape concentrate (16 fl. oz.)
   453 g. sugar (1 lb.)
   213 ml. rosepetals (7½ fl. oz.)
   or 1½ g. dried rosepetals
   1 tsp. malic acid
   ½ tsp. tartaric acid
   1 – 3 mg. Benerva tablet
   ¼ tsp. tannin
   1 tablet yeast nutrient
   ½ tsp. ammonium phosphate
   ½ tsp. yeast energiser
   yeast starter
   water to 4.55 litre (1 gal.)
Method:
Method A, but ignore all mention of 'other fruit'.

(22)

Ingredients:
680 g. green (ripe) elderberries (1½ lb).   W
1.7 litre apple juice, unsweetened (3 pint)
284 ml. white grape concentrate (½ pint)
453 g. honey (1 lb.)
113 ml. rosepetals (4 fl. oz.)
or 1 g. dried rosepetals
2 g. dried elderflowers
or 113 ml. elderflowers (4 fl. oz.)
1 tsp. malic acid
½ tsp. tartaric acid
1 – 3 mg. Benerva tablet   ½ tsp. yeast energiser
¼ tsp. tannin   yeast starter
1 tablet yeast nutrient   water to 4.55 litre (1 gal.)
½ tsp. ammonium phosphate   4 tsp. Pectozyme

Method:
Method A, ignoring all mention of 'other fruit'; add tannin at the same time as the yeast starter, and add the apple juice with the grape concentrate, together with the Pectozyme. It must be remembered to prepare the honey syrup as previously described.

(23)

Ingredients:
680 g. elderberries (1½ lb.)   W
907 g. apricots, canned (2 lb.)
284 ml. white grape concentrate (½ pint)
680 g. honey (1½ lb.)
213 ml. rosepetals (7½ fl. oz.)
or 1½ g. dried rosepetals   ½ tsp. ammonium phosphate
1 tsp. malic acid   ½ tsp. yeast energiser
½ tsp. tartaric acid   yeast starter
1 – 3 mg. Benerva tablet   water to 4.55 litre (1 gal.)
1 tablet yeast nutrient   2 tsp. Pectozyme

Method:
Method A, not forgetting the preparation of the honey syrup.

(24)

Ingredients:
680 g. green (ripe) elderberries (1½ lb.)   W
226 g. bananas (½ lb.)
426 ml. white grape concentrate (¾ pint)
570 g. sugar (1¼ lb.)
213 ml. rosepetals (7½ fl. oz.)
or 1½ g. dried rosepetals
1 tsp. malic acid
½ tsp. tartaric acid
1 – 3 mg. Benerva tablet
¼ tsp. tannin   ½ tsp. yeast energiser
1 tablet yeast nutrient   yeast starter
½ tsp. ammonium phosphate   water to 4.55 litre (1 gal.)
Method:
Method A, ignoring all mention of 'other fruit'; add tannin at the same time as the yeast starter. It will be remembered to prepare the banana syrup.

(25)

Ingredients:
680 g. elderberries (1½ lb.)   R
226 g. bananas (½ lb.)
426 ml. red grape concentrate (¾ pint)
570 g. sugar (1¼ lb.)
4 g. dried elderflowers
or 213 ml. elderflowers (7½ fl. oz.)
1 tsp. malic acid
½ tsp. tartaric acid
1 – 3 mg. Benerva tablet
1 tablet yeast nutrient
yeast starter
water to 4.55 litre (1 gal.)
Method:
Method A, ignoring all mention of 'other fruit'. The banana syrup will be prepared as previously described.

(26)

Ingredients:
  680 g. elderberries (1½ lb.)
  907 g. blackberries, canned (2 lb.)
  398 ml. red grape concentrate (14 fl. oz.)
  453 g. sugar (1 lb.)
  213 ml. rosepetals (7½ fl. oz.)
  or 1½ g. dried rosepetals
  1 tsp. malic acid
  ½ tsp. tartaric acid
  1 – 3 mg. Benerva tablet
  1 tablet yeast nutrient
  ½ tsp. ammonium phosphate
  ½ tsp. yeast energiser
  yeast starter
  water to 4.55 litre (1 gal.)
Method:
  Method A.

(27)

Ingredients:
  680 g. elderberries (1½ lb.)
  1.36 kg. cherries, canned (3 lb.)
  284 ml. red grape concentrate (½ pint)
  453 g. sugar (1 lb.)
  213 ml. rosepetals (7½ fl. oz.)
  or 1½ g. dried rosepetals
  1 tsp. malic acid
  ½ tsp. tartaric acid
  1 – 3 mg. Benerva tablet
  1 tablet yeast nutrient
  ½ tsp. ammonium phosphate
  ½ tsp. yeast energiser
  yeast starter
  water to 4.55 litre (1 gal.)
Method:
  Method A.

(28)

Ingredients:
680 g. green (ripe) elderberries (1½ lb.)   W
907 g. gooseberries, canned (2 lb.)
398 ml. white grape concentrate (14 fl. oz.)
453 g. sugar (1 lb.)
4 g. dried elderflowers
or 213 ml. elderflowers (7½ fl. oz.)
1 tsp. tartaric acid
1 – 3 mg. Benerva tablet
¼ tsp. tannin
1 tablet yeast nutrient
½ tsp. ammonium phosphate
½ tsp. yeast energiser
yeast starter
water to 4.55 litre (1 gal.)
2 tsp. Pectozyme
Method:
Method A

(29)

Ingredients: W
680 g. green (ripe) elderberries (1½ lb.)
907 g. gooseberries, canned (2 lb.)
284 ml. orange juice, unsweetened (½ pint)
284 ml. white grape concentrate (½ pint)
570 g. sugar (1¼ lb.)
4 g. dried elderflowers
or 213 ml. elderflowers (7½ fl. oz.)
1 tsp. tartaric acid
1 – 3 mg. Benerva tablet   ½ tsp. yeast energiser
¼ tsp. tannin   yeast starter
1 tablet yeast nutrient   water to 4.55 litre (1 gal.)
½ tsp. ammonium phosphate   2 tsp. Pectozyme
Method:
Method A, adding the orange juice at the same time as the 'other fruit', which in this case are gooseberries.

(30)

Ingredients:
  680 g. elderberries (1½ lb.)   R
  907 g. greengages, canned (2 lb.)
  284 ml. red grape concentrate (½ pint)
  570 g. sugar (1¼ lb.)
  4 g. dried elderflowers
  or 213 ml. elderflowers (7½ fl. oz.)
  1 tsp. malic acid
  ½ tsp. tartaric acid
  1 – 3 mg. Benerva tablet
  1 tablet yeast nutrient
  ½ tsp. ammonium phosphate
  ½ tsp. yeast energiser
  yeast starter
  water to 4.55 litre (1 gal.)
  2 tsp Pectozyme
Method:
  Method A.

(31)

Ingredients:
  680 g. green (ripe) elderberries (1½ lb.)   White
  568 ml. orange juice, unsweetened (1 pint)
  199 ml. white grape concentrate (7 fl. oz.)
  907 g. honey (2 lb.)
  213 ml. rosepetals (7½ fl. oz.)
  or 1½ g. dried rosepetals   1 tablet yeast nutrient
  ½ tsp. malic acid   ½ tsp. ammonium phosphate
  ½ tsp. tartaric acid   ½ tsp. yeast energiser
  1 – 3 mg. Benerva tablet   yeast starter
  ¼ tsp. tannin   water to 4.55 litre (1 gal.)
Method:
  Method A, ignoring all mention of 'other fruit', add tannin at the
same time as the yeast starter, and add the orange juice with the
grape concentrate, together with the Pectozyme. Honey syrup will
be prepared as previously described.

(32)

Ingredients:

680 g. green (ripe) elderberries (1½ lb.)   *white*
1.36 kg. parsnips (3 lb.)
284 ml. white grape concentrate (½ pint)
907 g. honey (2 lb.)
213 ml. rosepetals (7½ fl. oz.)
or 1½ g. dried rosepetals
1 tsp. malic acid
½ tsp. tartaric acid
1 – 3 mg. Benerva tablet
¼ tsp. tannin
1 tablet yeast nutrient
½ tsp. ammonium phosphate
½ tsp. yeast energiser
yeast starter
water to 4.55 litre (1 gal.)
3 tsp. Pectozyme

Method:

Method A, but for 'other fruit' read parsnip liquor – made by meticulously scrubbing the frosted parsnips absolutely clean, simmering the sliced pieces until tender, but not mushy (about ten minutes), and straining them off the liquor. The Pectozyme is required for the parsnips, all as described for the 'other fruit' in the standard method. The honey syrup is prepared as previously described under the section on Ingredients.

(33)

Ingredients:
   680 g. green (ripe) elderberries (1½ lb.)
   1.36 kg. peaches, canned (3 lb.)
   284 ml. white grape concentrate (½ pint) *white*
   680 g. honey (1½ lb.)
   213 ml. rosepetals (7½ fl. oz.)
   or 1½ g. dried rosepetals
   1 tsp. malic acid
   ½ tsp. tartaric acid
   1 – 3 mg. Benerva tablet
   ¼ tsp. tannin
   1 tablet yeast nutrient
   ½ tsp. ammonium phosphate
   ½ tsp. yeast energiser
   yeast starter
   water to 4.55 litre (1 gal.)
   3 tsp. Pectozyme
Method:
   Method A. The honey syrup is prepared as described under the
section on Ingredients.

(34)

Ingredients:
   680 g. elderberries (1½ lb.)   *white*
   1.36 kg. pears, canned (3 lb.)
   284 ml. white grape concentrate (½ pint)
   680 g. honey (1½ lb.)
   4 g. dried elderflowers
   or 213 ml. elderflowers (7½ fl. oz.)

1 tsp. malic acid	½ tsp. ammonium phosphate
½ tsp. tartaric acid	½ tsp. yeast energiser
1 – 3 mg. Benerva tablet	yeast starter
1 tablet yeast nutrient	water to 4.55 litre (1 gal.)

Method:
   Method A. The honey syrup is prepared as described under the
section on Ingredients.

(35)

Ingredients:
   680 g. elderberries (1½ lb.)
   907 g. plums, golden, canned (2 lb.)
   284 ml. white grape concentrate (½ pint)
   540 g. sugar (19 oz.)
   213 ml. rosepetals (7½ fl. oz.)
   or 1½ g. dried rosepetals
   1 tsp. malic acid
   ½ tsp. tartaric acid   ½ tsp. yeast energiser
   1 – 3 mg. Benerva tablet   yeast starter
   1 tablet yeast nutrient   water to 4.55 litre (1 gal.)
   ½ tsp. ammonium phosphate   2 tsp. Pectozyme
Method:
   Method A.

(36)

Ingredients:
   680 g. green (ripe) elderberries (1½ lb.)   *white*
   1.36 kg. rhubarb, canned (3 lb.)
   284 ml. white grape concentrate (½ pint)
   680 g. honey (1½ lb.)
   4 g. dried elderflowers
   or 213 ml. elderflowers (7½ fl. oz.)
   1 tsp. malic acid
   ½ tsp. tartaric acid   ½ tsp. amm. phosphate
   1 – 3 mg. Benerva tablet   ½ tsp. yeast energiser
   ¼ tsp. tannin   yeast starter
   1 tablet yeast nutrient   water to 4.55 litre (1 gal.)
Method:
   Method A. The rhubarb is treated with small doses of precipitated chalk (calcium carbonate), until the fizzing is almost non-existent, before the Campden tablets are added – this to remove the oxalic acid. The honey syrup is prepared as described under the section on Ingredients.

61

(37)

Ingredients:
  680 g. green (ripe) elderberries (1½ lb.) *White*
  341 ml. rosehip syrup, bottled (12 fl. oz.)
  284 ml. white grape concentrate (½ pint)
  453 g. honey (1 lb.)
  213 ml. rosepetals (7½ fl. oz.)
  or 1½ g. dried rosepetals
  1 tsp. malic acid
  ½ tsp. tartaric acid
  1 – 3 mg. Benerva tablet
  ¼ tsp. tannin   ½ tsp. yeast energiser
  1 tablet yeast nutrient   yeast starter
  ½ tsp. ammonium phosphate   water to 4.55 litre (1 gal.)

Method:
  Method A, ignoring all mention of 'other fruit'; add tannin at the same time as the yeast starter, and add the rosehip syrup with the grape concentrate. Honey syrup is prepared as described under the section on Ingredients.

SPARKLING TABLE

(38)

Ingredients:
  284 ml. elderflowers (white, not cream-coloured) (½ pint)
  1.02 kg. honey (2¼ lb.)
  ½ tsp. citric acid
  1 tsp. malic acid
  ½ tsp. tartaric acid
  ¼ tsp. tannin
  1 – 3 mg. Benerva tablet
  1 tablet yeast nutrient
  ½ tsp. ammonium phosphate
  ½ tsp. yeast energiser
  yeast starter
  water to 4.55 litre (1 gal.)

Method:
1st Day – Prepare the yeast starter.
2nd Day – Simmer the honey in its own volume of water for ten minutes, and cool in a container to 21°C (70°F).
4th Day – Add the flowers contained in a filter bag.
7th Day – Take out the flowers, funnel the liquor into a demijohn, top up with warm water if necessary, fit holed bung and part water-filled fermentation lock, and keep at 21°C (70°F).
11th Day – Proceed as for 15th day of Method D.

(39)

Ingredients:
142 ml. elderflowers, white (¼ pint)
142 ml. rosepetals (¼ pint)
795 g. sugar (1¾ lb.)
½ tsp. citric acid
1 tsp. malic acid
½ tsp. tartaric acid
¼ tsp. tannin
1 – 3 mg. Benerva tablet
1 tablet yeast nutrient
½ tsp. ammonium phosphate
½ tsp. yeast energiser
yeast starter
water to 4.55 litre (1 gal.)

Method:
1st Day – Prepare the yeast starter.
2nd Day – Invert the sugar by simmering it with one teaspoonful of citric acid in 568 ml. (one pint) of water until it is straw-coloured. Cool to 21°C (70°F) in a container, add the other ingredients, including the yeast starter but not the flowers, fill to the 4.55 litre (one gallon) mark with boiled, cooled and aerated water, cover, and keep at 21°C (70°F).
4th Day – Add the flowers contained in a filter bag.
7th Day – Take out the flowers, funnel the liquor into a demijohn, top up with warm water if necessary, fit holed bung and part water-filled fermentation lock, and keep at 21°C (70°F).
11th Day – Proceed as for 15th day of Method D.

(40)

Ingredients:
284 ml. elderflowers, white (½ pint)
568 ml. white grape concentrate (1 pint)
340 g. sugar (¾ lb.)   1 tablet yeast nutrient
¼ tsp. citric acid   ½ tsp. ammonium phosphate
½ tsp. malic acid   ½ tsp. yeast energiser
¼ tsp. tartaric acid   yeast starter
1 – 3 mg. Benerva tablet   water to 4.55 litre (1 gal.)

Method:
1st Day – Prepare the yeast starter.

2nd Day – Invert the sugar by simmering it with one teaspoonful of citric acid in 284 ml. (½ pint) water until it is straw-coloured. Cool to 21°C (70°F) in a container, add the other ingredients, including the yeast starter but not the flowers, fill to the 4.55 litre (one gallon) mark with boiled, cooled and aerated water, cover, and keep at 21°C (70°F).

4th Day – Add the flowers contained in a filter bag.

7th Day – Take out the flowers, funnel the liquor into a demijohn, top up with warm water if necessary, fit holed bung and part water-filled fermentation lock, and keep at 21°C (70°F).

11th Day – Proceed as for 15th day of Method D.

(41)

Ingredients:
142 ml. elderflowers, white (¼ pint)
142 ml. rosepetals, white (¼ pint)
453 g. fruit cocktail, canned (1 lb.)
199 ml. white grape concentrate (7 fl. oz.)
570 g. sugar (1¼ lb.)
¼ tsp. citric acid   ½ tsp. ammonium phosphate
½ tsp. malic acid   ½ tsp. yeast energiser
¼ tsp. tartaric acid   yeast starter
1 – 3 mg. Benerva tablet   water to 4.55 litre (1 gal.)
1 tablet yeast nutrient   1 tsp. Pectozyme

Method:
Method E.

(42)

Ingredients:
 284 ml. elderflowers, white (½ pint)
 115 g. strawberries, canned (¼ lb.)
 398 ml. white grape concentrate (14 fl. oz.)
 453 g. sugar (1 lb.)
 ¼ tsp. citric acid
 ½ tsp. malic acid
 ¼ tsp. tartaric acid
 1 – 3 mg. Benerva tablet
 1 tablet yeast nutrient
 ½ tsp. ammonium phosphate
 ½ tsp. yeast energiser
 yeast starter
 water to 4.55 litre (1 gal.)
Method:
 Method E.

(43)

Ingredients:
 453 g. elderberries (1 lb.)
 795 g. sugar (1¾ lb.)
 3 g. dried elderflowers
 or 142 ml. elderflowers (5 fl. oz.)
 ½ tsp. malic acid
 ¼ tsp. tartaric acid
 1 – 3 mg. Benerva tablet
 1 tablet yeast nutrient
 ½ tsp. ammonium phosphate
 ½ tsp. yeast energiser
 yeast starter
 water to 4.55 litre (1 gal.)
Method:
 Method D, ignoring all mention of 'other fruit'. The sugar to be
inverted as described in the Ingredients section.

(44)

Ingredients:
453 g. elderberries (1 lb.)
284 ml. red grape concentrate (½ pint)
570 g. sugar (1¼ lb.)
3 g. dried elderflowers
or 142 ml. elderflowers (5 fl. oz.)
½ tsp. malic acid
¼ tsp. tartaric acid
1 – 3 mg. Benerva tablet   ½ tsp. yeast energiser
1 tablet yeast nutrient   yeast starter
½ tsp. ammonium phosphate   water to 4.55 litre (1 gal.)
Method:
As for Method D, ignoring all mention of 'other fruit'. The sugar
to be inverted as described in the Ingredients section.

(45)

Ingredients:
453 g. green (ripe) elderberries (1 lb.)
284 ml. white grape concentrate (½ pint)
680 g. honey (1½ lb.)
142 ml. rosepetals (¼ pint)
or 1 g. dried rosepetals
½ tsp. malic acid
¼ tsp. tartaric acid
¼ tsp. tannin
1 – 3 mg. Benerva tablet
1 tablet yeast nutrient
½ tsp. ammonium phosphate
½ tsp. yeast energiser
yeast starter
water to 4.55 litre (1 gal.)
Method:
Method D, ignoring all mention of 'other fruit'. The honey syrup
to be prepared as described under the Ingredients section.

(46)

Ingredients:
  453 g. elderberries (1 lb.)
  1.36 kg. apples, canned (3 lb.)
  142 ml. white grape concentrate (¼ pint)
  625 g. sugar (22 oz.)
  142 ml. rosepetals (¼ pint)
  or 1 g. dried rosepetals
  ½ tsp. malic acid
  ¼ tsp. tartaric acid
  1 – 3 mg. Benerva tablet
  1 tablet yeast nutrient
  ½ tsp. ammonium phosphate
  ½ tsp. yeast energiser
  yeast starter
  water to 4.55 litre (1 gal.)
  3 tsp. Pectozyme
Method:
  Method D. The sugar to be inverted as previously described.

(47)

Ingredients:
  453 g. green (ripe) elderberries (1 lb.)
  1.36 kg. apricots, canned (3 lb.)
  142 ml. white grape concentrate (¼ pint)
  600 g. honey (21 oz.)
  142 ml. rosepetals (¼ pint)
  or 1 g. dried rosepetals
  ½ tsp. malic acid   ½ tsp. ammonium phosphate
  ¼ tsp. tartaric acid   ½ tsp. yeast energiser
  1 – 3 mg. Benerva tablet   yeast starter
  ¼ tsp. tannin   water to 4.55 litre (1 gal.)
  1 tablet yeast nutrient   3 tsp. Pectozyme
Method:
  Method D. The honey syrup to be produced as described in the section on Ingredients.

(48)

Ingredients:
453 g. elderberries (1 lb.)
453 g. bilberry pie filling, canned (1 lb.)
199 ml. white grape concentrate (7 fl. oz.)
570 g. sugar (1¼ lb.)
3 g. dried elderflowers
or 142 ml. elderflowers (¼ pint)
½ tsp. malic acid
¼ tsp. tartaric acid
1 – 3 mg. Benerva tablet
1 tablet yeast nutrient
½ tsp. ammonium phosphate
½ tsp. yeast energiser
yeast starter
water to 4.55 litre (1 gal.)
1 tsp. Pectozyme
Method:
Method D. The sugar to be inverted as described in the
Ingredients section.

(49)

Ingredients:
453 g. elderberries (1 lb.)
453 g. cherries, canned (1 lb.)
199 ml. red grape concentrate (7 fl. oz.)
570 g. sugar (1¼ lb.)
3 g. dried elderflowers
or 142 ml. elderflowers (¼ pint)
½ tsp. malic acid
¼ tsp. tartaric acid
1 – 3 mg. Benerva tablet   ½ tsp. yeast energiser
1 tablet yeast nutrient   yeast starter
½ tsp. ammonium phosphate   water to 4.55 litre (1 gal.)
Method:
Method D. The sugar to be inverted as described in the
Ingredients section.

(50)

Ingredients:
453 g. green (ripe) elderberries (1 lb.)
1.36 kg. gooseberries, canned (3 lb.)
142 ml. white grape concentrate (¼ pint)
510 g. sugar (18 oz.)
142 ml. rosepetals (¼ pint)
or 1 g. dried rosepetals
¼ tsp. tartaric acid
1 – 3 mg. Benerva tablet
¼ tsp. tannin
1 tablet yeast nutrient
½ tsp. ammonium phosphate
½ tsp. yeast energiser
yeast starter
water to 4.55 litre (1 gal.)
3 tsp. Pectozyme

Method:
Method D. The sugar to be inverted as described in the Ingredients section.

(51)

Ingredients:
453 g. elderberries (1 lb.)
284 ml. grapefruit juice, canned (10 fl. oz.)
142 ml. white grape concentrate (5. fl. oz.)
740 g. honey (26 oz.)
3 g. dried elderflowers
or 142 ml. elderflowers (¼ pint)   ½ tsp. amm. phosphate
½ tsp. tartaric acid   ½ tsp. yeast energiser
1 – 3 mg. Benerva tablet   yeast starter
1 tablet yeast nutrient   water to 4.55 litre (1 gal.)

Method:
Method D. The honey syrup to be prepared as described in the Ingredients section.

(52)

Ingredients:
453 g. elderberries (1 lb.)
115 g. loganberries, canned (¼ lb.)
284 ml. red grape concentrate (½ pint)
453 g. sugar (1 lb.)
142 ml. rosepetals (¼ pint)
or 1 g. dried rosepetals
½ tsp. malic acid
¼ tsp. tartaric acid
1 – 3 mg. Benerva tablet
1 tablet yeast nutrient
½ tsp. ammonium phosphate
½ tsp. yeast energiser
yeast starter
water to 4.55 litre (1 gal.)
¼ tsp. Pectozyme
Method:
Method D. The sugar to be inverted as described in the Ingredients section.

(53)

Ingredients:
453 g. green (ripe) elderberries (1 lb.)
284 ml. orange juice, unsweetened (½ pint)
142 ml. white grape concentrate (¼ pint)
795 g. honey (1¾ lb.)
3 g. dried elderflowers
or 142 ml. elderflowers (¼ pint)   1 tablet yeast nutrient
½ tsp. malic acid   ½ tsp. amm. phosphate
¼ tsp. tartaric acid   ½ tsp. yeast energiser
¼ tsp. tannin   yeast starter
1 – 3 mg. Benerva tablet   water to 4.55 litre (1 gal.)
Method:
Method D. The honey syrup to be prepared as described in the Ingredients section.

70

(54)

Ingredients:
453 g. green (ripe) elderberries (1 lb.)
907 g. peaches, canned (2 lb.)
142 ml. white grape concentrate (¼ pint)
570 g. sugar (1¼ lb.)
142 ml. rosepetals (¼ pint)
or 1 g. dried rosepetals
½ tsp. malic acid
¼ tsp. tartaric acid
1 – 3 mg. Benerva tablet
¼ tsp. tannin
1 tablet yeast nutrient
½ tsp. ammonium phosphate
½ tsp. yeast energiser
yeast starter
water to 4.55 litre (1 gal.)
2 tsp. Pectozyme
Method:
Method D. The sugar to be inverted as described in the
Ingredients section.

(55)

Ingredients:
453 g. elderberries (1 lb.)
1.36 kg. pears, canned
142 ml. white grape concentrate (¼ pint)
510 g. sugar (18 oz.)
142 ml. rosepetals (¼ pint)   1 tablet yeast nutrient
or 1 g. dried rosepetals   ½ tsp. ammonium phosphate
½ tsp. malic acid   ½ tsp. yeast energiser
¼ tsp. tartaric acid   yeast starter
1 – 3 mg. Benerva tablet   water to 4.55 litre (1 gal.)
Method:
Method D. The sugar to be inverted as described in the
Ingredients section.

(56)

Ingredients:
  453 g. elderberries (1 lb.)
  142 ml. raspberries, canned (¼ pint)
  199 ml. white grape concentrate (7 fl. oz.)
  570 g. sugar (1¼ lb.)
  3 g. dried elderflowers
  or 142 ml. elderflowers (¼ pint)
  ½ tsp. malic acid
  ¼ tsp. tartaric acid
  1 – 3 mg. Benerva tablet
  1 tablet yeast nutrient
  ½ tsp. ammonium phosphate
  ½ tsp. yeast energiser
  yeast starter
  water to 4.55 litre (1 gal.)
  ½ tsp. Pectozyme
Method:
Method D. The sugar to be inverted as described in the Ingredients section.

(57)

Ingredients:
  453 g. elderberries (1 lb.)
  907 g. rhubarb, canned (2 lb.)
  199 ml. white grape concentrate (7 fl. oz.)
  453 g. sugar (1 lb.)   1 – 3 mg. Benerva tablet
  3 g. dried elderflowers   1 tablet yeast nutrient
  or 142 ml. elderflowers (¼ pint)   ½ tsp. amm. phosphate
  ½ tsp. malic acid   ½ tsp. yeast energiser
  ¼ tsp. tartaric acid   yeast starter
Method: water to 4.55 litre (1 gal.)

Method D. The rhubarb to be treated with small doses of precipitated chalk (calcium carbonate) until the fizzing is almost non-existent, and before the Campden tablets are added, in order to remove the oxalic acid. The sugar is to be inverted as described in the Ingredients section.

(58)

Ingredients:
453 g. elderberries (1 lb.)
170 ml. Ribena syrup (6 fl. oz.)
284 ml. red grape concentrate (½ pint)
453 g. sugar (1 lb.)
3 g. dried elderflowers
or 142 ml. elderflowers (¼ pint)
½ tsp. malic acid   ½ tsp. yeast energiser
1 – 3 mg. Benerva tablet   yeast starter
1 tablet yeast nutrient   water to 4.55 litre (1 gal.)
½ tsp. ammonium phosphate   ½ tsp. Pectozyme

Method:
Method D, ignoring all mention of the 'other fruit'. Add the Ribena with the grape concentrate, together with the Pectozyme. The sugar to be inverted as described in the Ingredients section.

(59)

Ingredients:
453 g. green (ripe) elderberries (1 lb.)
284 ml. tangerine juice (10 fl. oz.)
142 ml. white grape concentrate (5 fl. oz.)
570 g. sugar (1¼ lb.)
142 ml. rosepetals (¼ pint)
or 1 g. dried rosepetals
½ tsp. malic acid
¼ tsp. tartaric acid
1 – 3 mg. Benerva tablet
¼ tsp. tannin
1 tablet yeast nutrient
½ tsp. ammonium phosphate
½ tsp. yeast energiser
yeast starter
water to 4.55 litre (1 gal.)

Method:
Method D, but ignore all references to the 'other fruit'. Add the tangerine juice on the fifth day. Invert the sugar.

(60)

Ingredients:

453 g. green (ripe) elderberries (1 lb.)
1.14 kg. vine prunings (2½ lb.)
142 ml. white grape concentrate (¼ pint)
625 g. sugar (22 oz.)
142 ml. rosepetals (¼ pint)
or 1 g. dried rosepetals
½ tsp. malic acid
¼ tsp. tartaric acid
¼ tsp. tannin
1 – 3 mg. Benerva tablet
1 tablet yeast nutrient
½ tsp. ammonium phosphate
½ tsp. yeast energiser
yeast starter
water to 4.55 litre (1 gal.)
1 tsp. Pectozyme

Method:

As Method D but ignore all references to the 'other fruit', and prepare the vine prunings liquor ready for addition to the fermentation on the fifth day. At the same time as the yeast starter is prepared, (on the second day), wash the vine prunings, chop them up into pieces about 5 cm. (2 in.) long, simmer in 1.7 litre (3 pint) of water for half an hour, stirring them up frequently, cool to room temperature in a container, add 2 Campden tablets and the Pectozyme, and leave covered for 3 days; strain, press out, and add the liquor to the fermentation. The sugar is inverted as described in the section on Ingredients.

DESSERT

(61)

Ingredients:
1.36 kg. elderberries (3 lb.)
2.27 kg. apples, canned (5 lb.)
453 g. blackcurrants, canned (1 lb.)
226 g. bananas (½ lb.)
426 ml. red grape concentrate (¾ pint)
680 g. sugar (1½ lb.)
8 g. dried elderflowers
or 426 ml. elderflowers (¾ pint)
2 tsp. malic acid
2 tsp. tartaric acid
1 – 3 mg. Benerva tablet
1 tablet yeast nutrient   yeast starter
½ tsp. ammonium phosphate   water to 4.55 litre (1 gal.)
½ tsp. yeast energiser   6 tsp. Pectozyme
Method:
Method C.

(62)

Ingredients:
1.36 kg. green (ripe) elderberries (3 lb.)
1.36 kg. apricots, canned (3 lb.)
907 g. bananas (2 lb.)
568 ml. white grape concentrate (1 pint)
680 g. sugar (1½ lb.)   1 tablet yeast nutrient
8 g. dried elderflowers   ½ tsp. ammonium phosphate
or 426 ml. elderflowers (¾ pint)
2 tsp. malic acid   ½ tsp. yeast energiser
2 tsp. tartaric acid   yeast starter
1 – 3 mg. Benerva tablet   water to 4.55 litre (1 gal.)
1 tsp. tannin   3 tsp. Pectozyme
Method:
Method C.

(63)

Ingredients:
1.36 kg. elderberries (3 lb.)
453 g. bananas (1 lb.)
852 ml. red grape concentrate (1½ pint)
625 g. sugar (22 oz.)
426 ml. rosepetals (¾ pint)
or 3 g. dried rosepetals
2 tsp. malic acid
2 tsp. tartaric acid
1 – 3 mg. Benerva tablet
1 tablet yeast nutrient
½ tsp. ammonium phosphate
½ tsp. yeast energiser
yeast starter
water to 4.55 litre (1 gal.)

Method:
Method C, but ignore all references to the 'other fruit'.

(64)

Ingredients:
1.36 kg. elderberries (3 lb.)
1.36 kg. bilberry pie filling (3 lb.)
680 g. bananas (1½ lb.)
568 ml. red grape concentrate (1 pint)
907 g. honey (2 lb.)
8 g. dried elderflowers
or 426 ml. elderflowers (¾ pint)
2 tsp. malic acid
2 tsp. tartaric acid
1 – 3 mg. Benerva tablet
1 tablet yeast nutrient
½ tsp. ammonium phosphate
½ tsp. yeast energiser
yeast starter
water to 4.55 litre (1 gal.)
3 tsp. Pectozyme

Method:
Method C.

(65)

Ingredients:
1.36 kg. green (ripe) elderberries (3 lb.)
1.36 kg. blackberry & apple pie filling
907 g. bananas (2 lb.)
568 ml. white grape concentrate (1 pint)
680 g. sugar (1½ lb.)
426 ml. rosepetals (¾ pint)
or 3 g. dried rosepetals
2 tsp. malic acid
2 tsp. tartaric acid
1 – 3 mg. Benerva tablet   ½ tsp. yeast energiser
1 tsp. tannin   yeast starter
1 tablet yeast nutrient   water to 4.55 litre (1 gal.)
½ tsp. ammonium phosphate   2 tsp. Pectozyme
Method:
Method C.

(66)

Ingredients:
1.36 kg. elderberries (3 lb.)
1.36 kg. blackberries, canned (3 lb.)
680 g. bananas (1½ lb.)
568 ml. red grape concentrate (1 pint)
680 g. sugar (1½ lb.)
426 ml. rosepetals (¾ pint)
or 3 g. dried rosepetals
2 tsp. malic acid
2 tsp. tartaric acid
1 – 3 mg. Benerva tablet
1 tablet yeast nutrient
½ tsp. ammonium phosphate   yeast starter
½ tsp. yeast energiser   water to 4.55 litre (1 gal.)
Method:
Method C.

(67)

Ingredients:
  1.36 kg. elderberries (3 lb.)
  1.14 kg. blackberries, canned (2½ lb.)
  1.14 kg. greengages, canned (2½ lb.)
  907 g. bananas (2 lb.)
  426 ml. white grape concentrate (¾ pint)
  680 g. sugar (1½ lb.)
  426 ml. rosepetals (¾ pint)
  or 3 g. dried rosepetals
  2 tsp. malic acid
  2 tsp. tartaric acid   ½ tsp. yeast energiser
  1 – 3 mg. Benerva tablet   yeast starter
  1 tablet yeast nutrient   water to 4.55 litre (1 gal.)
  ½ tsp. ammonium phosphate   2 tsp. Pectozyme
Method:
  Method C.

(68)

Ingredients:
  1.36 kg. green (ripe) elderberries (3 lb.)
  1.36 kg. gooseberries, canned (3 lb.)
  907 g. bananas (2 lb.)
  568 ml. white grape concentrate (1 pint)
  680 g. sugar (1½ lb.)
  426 ml. rosepetals (¾ pint)
  or 3 g. dried rosepetals
  1 tsp. malic acid
  2 tsp. tartaric acid
  1 – 3 mg. Benerva tablet
  1 tsp. tannin
  1 tablet yeast nutrient   yeast starter
  ½ tsp. ammonium phosphate   water to 4.55 litre (1 gal.)
  ½ tsp. yeast energiser   3 tsp. Pectozyme
Method:
  Method C.

(69)

Ingredients:
1.36 kg. elderberries (3 lb.)
1.7 litre orange juice, unsweetened (3 pint)
453 g. bananas (1 lb.)
568 ml. white grape concentrate (1 pint)
795 g. sugar (1¾ lb.)
426 ml. rosepetals (¾ pint)
or 3 g. dried rosepetals
2 tsp. malic acid
2 tsp. tartaric acid
1 – 3 mg. Benerva tablet   ½ tsp. yeast energiser
1 tablet yeast nutrient   yeast starter
½ tsp. ammonium phosphate   water to 4.55 litre (1 gal.)

Method:

Method C, but ignore all references to the 'other fruit' and add the orange juice to the must on the fifth day.

(70)

Ingredients:
1.36 kg. green (ripe) elderberries (3 lb.)
1.82 kg. parsnips (4 lb.)
453 g. bananas (1 lb.)
568 ml. white grape concentrate (1 pint)
795 g. sugar (1¾ lb.)
8 g. dried elderflowers
or 426 ml. elderflowers
2 tsp. malic acid
2 tsp. tartaric acid
1 – 3 mg. Benerva tablet
1 tsp. tannin
1 tablet yeast nutrient
½ tsp. ammonium phosphate
½ tsp. yeast energiser
yeast starter
water to 4.55 litre (1 gal.)
4 tsp. Pectozyme

Method:

Method C, but for 'other fruit' read parsnips, and add the prepared parsnip juice together with the Pectozyme to the must on the fifth day – to prepare the parsnip juice, scrub the frosted parsnips absolutely clean, simmer the sliced pieces until absolutely tender, but not mushy (about ten minutes), and strain them off the liquor.

(71)

Ingredients:

1.36 kg. green (ripe) elderberries (3 lb.)
1.82 kg. peaches, canned (4 lb.)
907 g. bananas (2 lb.)
426 ml. white grape concentrate (¾ pint)
907 g. honey (2 lb.)
426 ml. rosepetals (¾ pint)
or 3 g. dried rosepetals
2 tsp. malic acid
2 tsp. tartaric acid
1 – 3 mg. Benerva tablet
1 tsp. tannin
1 tablet yeast nutrient
½ tsp. ammonium phosphate
½ tsp. yeast energiser
yeast starter
water to 4.55 litre (1 gal.)
4 tsp. Pectozyme

Method:

Method C, but prepare the banana and honey syrups as described under the section on Ingredients.

(72)

Ingredients:
   1.36 kg. elderberries (3 lb.)
   907 g. peaches, canned (2 lb.)
   453 g. bilberries, canned (1 lb.)
   710 ml. white grape concentrate (25 fl. oz.)
   680 g. sugar (1½ lb.)
   8 g. dried elderflowers
   or 426 ml. elderflowers (¾ pint)
   2 tsp. malic acid
   2 tsp. tartaric acid   ½ tsp. yeast energiser
   1 – 3 mg. Benerva tablet   yeast starter
   1 tablet yeast nutrient   water to 4.55 litre (1 gal.)
   ½ tsp. ammonium phosphate   3 tsp. Pectozyme
Method:
   Method C.

(73)

Ingredients:
   1.36 kg. elderberries (3 lb.)
   1.36 kg. pears, canned (3 lb.)
   453 g. bananas (1 lb.)
   568 ml. red grape concentrate (1 pint)
   907 g. honey (2 lb.)
   426 ml. rosepetals (¾ pint)
   or 3 g. dried rosepetals
   2 tsp. tartaric acid
   1 – 3 mg. Benerva tablet
   1 tablet yeast nutrient
   ½ tsp. ammonium phosphate
   ½ tsp. yeast energiser
   yeast starter
   water to 4.55 litre (1 gal.)
Method:
   Method C. Prepare the banana and honey syrups as described
under the section on Ingredients.

(74)

Ingredients:
1.36 kg. elderberries (3 lb.)
1.82 kg. plums, golden, canned (4 lb.)
453 g. bananas (1 lb.)
568 ml. red grape concentrate (1 pint)
680 g. sugar (1½ lb.)
8 g. dried elderflowers
or 426 ml. elderflowers (¾ pint)
2 tsp. malic acid
2 tsp. tartaric acid   ½ tsp. yeast energiser
1 – 3 mg. Benerva tablet   yeast starter
1 tablet yeast nutrient   water to 4.55 litre (1 gal.)
½ tsp. amm. phosphate   4 tsp. Pectozyme
Method:
Method C. Prepare the banana syrup as described in the section under Ingredients.

(75)

Ingredients:
1.36 kg. elderberries (3 lb.)
226 g. raspberries, canned (½ lb.)
680 g. bananas (1½ lb.)
795 ml. red grape concentrate (28 fl. oz.)
625 g. sugar (22 oz.)
426 ml. rosepetals (¾ pint)
or 3 g. dried rosepetals
2 tsp. malic acid
2 tsp. tartaric acid   ½ tsp. yeast energiser
1 – 3 mg. Benerva tablet   yeast starter
1 tablet yeast nutrient   water to 4.55 litre (1 gal.)
½ tsp. ammonium phosphate   ½ tsp. Pectozyme
Method:
Method C. Prepare the banana syrup as described in the section under Ingredients.

(76)

Ingredients:
1.36 kg. elderberries (3 lb.)
326 ml. ribena syrup (11½ fl. oz. bottle)
907 g. bananas (2 lb.)
426 ml. red grape concentrate (¾ pint)
680 g. sugar (1½ lb.)
8 g. dried elderflowers
or 426 ml. elderflowers (¾ pint)
1 tsp. malic acid
1 tsp. tartaric acid   ½ tsp. yeast energiser
1 – 3 mg. Benerva tablet   yeast starter
1 tablet yeast nutrient   water to 4.55 litre (1 gal.)
½ tsp. ammonium phosphate   5 tsp. Pectozyme

Method:

Method C but ignore all references to the 'other fruit' and add the Ribena to the must on the fifth day, together with the Pectozyme.

(77)

Ingredients:
1.36 kg. elderberries (3 lb.)
341 ml. rosehip syrup (12 fl. oz.)
680 g. bananas (1½ lb.)
426 ml. red grape concentrate (¾ pint)
680 g. sugar (1½ lb.)
426 ml. rosepetals (¾ pint)
or 3 g. dried rosepetals
1½ tsp. malic acid   ½ tsp. amm. phosphate
1½ tsp. tartaric acid   ½ tsp. yeast energiser
1 – 3 mg. Benerva tablet   yeast starter
1 tablet yeast nutrient   water to 4.55 litre (1 gal.)

Method:

Method C, but ignore all references to the 'other fruit', and add the rosehip syrup on the fifth day.

SOCIAL

(78)

Ingredients:
  284 ml. elderflowers, white (½ pint)
  142 ml. rosepetals, red (¼ pint)
  907 g. blackcurrants, canned (2 lb.)
  795 ml. red grape concentrate (28 fl. oz.)
  570 g. sugar (1¼ lb.)
  1½ tsp. malic acid
  1½ tsp. tartaric acid
  1 – 3 mg. Benerva tablet
  1 tablet yeast nutrient
  ½ tsp. ammonium phosphate
  ½ tsp. yeast energiser
  yeast starter
  water to 4.55 litre (1 gal.)
  2 tsp. Pectozyme
Method:
  Method B.

(79)

Ingredients:
  426 ml. elderflowers (¾ pint)
  56 g. root ginger (2 oz.)
  1.14 litre white grape concentrate (1 quart)
  340 g. demerara sugar (¾ lb.)
  1 tsp. citric acid
  1½ tsp. malic acid
  1½ tsp. tartaric acid
  1 – 3 mg. Benerva tablet
  ¼ tsp. tannin
  1 tablet yeast nutrient
  ½ tsp. ammonium phosphate
  ½ tsp. yeast energiser
  yeast starter
  water to 4.55 litre (1 gal.)

Method:
1st Day – Prepare the yeast starter.

2nd Day – Thoroughly bruise the ginger, retaining it in a linen bag whilst wielding the hammer. Simmer the bruised ginger, sugar and citric acid in 284 ml. (½ pint) water for 20 minutes (remember that the acid will react on metal – use unchipped enamel). Remove the ginger, squeeze out, and when the liquor is cool add to the grape concentrate and all the other ingredients (except the elderflowers) contained in a white plastic bucket. Make up to the 4.55 litre (one gallon) mark with cool, boiled and aerated water, and add the yeast starter; cover and keep at 21°C (70°F).

7th Day – Add the flowers contained in a filter bag.

10th Day – Take out the flowers, funnel the liquor into a demijohn, top up with warm water if necessary, fit holed bung and part water-filled fermentation lock, and keep at 21°C (70°F).

15th Day – Proceed as for Method A.

(80)

Ingredients:
1.14 kg. elderberries (2½ lb.)
1.25 kg. sugar (2¾ lb.)
7 g. dried elderflowers
or 341 ml. elderflowers (12 fl. oz.)
1½ tsp. malic acid
1½ tsp. tartaric acid
1 – 3 mg. Benerva tablet
1 tablet yeast nutrient
½ tsp. ammonium phosphate
½ tsp. yeast energiser
yeast starter
water to 4.55 litre (1 gal.)

Method:
Method A, ignoring all mention of 'other fruit' and of the grape concentrate.

(81)

Ingredients:
  1.14 kg. elderberries (2½ lb.)
  795 ml. grape concentrate (28 fl. oz.)
  570 g. demerara sugar (1¼ lb.)
  341 ml. rosepetals (12 fl. oz.)
  or 2½ g. dried rosepetals
  1½ tsp. malic acid
  1½ tsp. tartaric acid
  1 – 3 mg. Benerva tablet
  1 tablet yeast nutrient
  ½ tsp. ammonium phosphate
  ½ tsp. yeast energiser
  yeast starter
  water to 4.55 litre (1 gal.)
Method:
  Method A, ignoring all mention of the 'other fruit'.

(82)

Ingredients:
  1.14 kg. elderberries (2½ lb.)
  1.36 kg. apple, canned pulp (3 lb.)
  568 ml. white grape concentrate (1 pint)
  570 g. sugar (1¼ lb.)
  341 ml. rosepetals (12 fl. oz.)
  or 2½ g. dried rosepetals
  1½ tsp. malic acid
  1½ tsp. tartaric acid
  1 – 3 mg. Benerva tablet
  1 tablet yeast nutrient
  ½ tsp. ammonium phosphate
  ½ tsp. yeast energiser
  yeast starter
  water to 4.55 litre (1 gal.)
  3 tsp. Pectozyme
Method:
  Method A.

(83)

Ingredients:
1.14 kg. green (ripe) elderberries (2½ lb.)
2.27 kg. apples, canned pulp (5 lb.)
426 ml. orange juice, unsweetened (¾ pint)
142 ml. white grape concentrate (¼ pint)
795 g. sugar (1¾ lb.)
341 ml. rosepetals (12 fl. oz.)
or 2½ g. dried rosepetals
1½ tsp. malic acid
1½ tsp. tartaric acid
1 – 3 mg. Benerva tablet
½ tsp. tannin
1 tablet yeast nutrient
½ tsp. ammonium phosphate
½ tsp. yeast energiser
yeast starter
water to 4.55 litre (1 gal.)
5 tsp. Pectozyme
Method:
Method A. Add the orange juice with the grape concentrate.

(84)

Ingredients:
1.14 kg. elderberries (2½ lb.)
453 g. apricot, canned (1 lb.)
795 ml. white grape concentrate (28 fl. oz.)
570 g. honey (1¼ lb.)
341 ml. rosepetals (12 fl. oz.)
or 2½ g. dried rosepetals   ½ tsp. ammonium phosphate
1½ tsp. malic acid   ½ tsp. yeast energiser
1½ tsp. tartaric acid   yeast starter
1 – 3 mg. Benerva tablet   water to 4.55 litre (1 gal.)
1 tablet yeast nutrient   1 tsp. Pectozyme
Method:
Method A. The honey syrup to be made as described under the
section on Ingredients.

(85)

Ingredients:
  1.14 kg. elderberries (2½ lb.)
  453 g. bananas (1 lb.)
  1.14 kg. sugar (2½ lb.)
  7 g. dried elderflowers
  or 341 ml. elderflowers (12 fl. oz.)
  1½ tsp. malic acid
  1½ tsp. tartaric acid
  1 – 3 mg. Benerva tablet
  1 tablet yeast nutrient
  ½ tsp. ammonium phosphate
  ½ tsp. yeast energiser
  yeast starter
  water to 4.55 litre (1 gal.)
Method:
Method A, ignoring all mention of the 'other fruit'. The banana
syrup to be prepared as described under the Ingredients section.

(86)

Ingredients:
  1.14 kg. green (ripe) elderberries (2½ lb.)
  453 g. bananas (1 lb.)
  568 ml. white grape concentrate (1 pint)
  907 g. honey (2 lb.)
  341 ml. rosepetals (12 fl. oz.)
  or 2½ g. dried rosepetals
  1½ tsp. malic acid
  1½ tsp. tartaric acid   ½ tsp. ammonium phosphate
  1 – 3 mg. Benerva tablet   ½ tsp. yeast energiser
  ½ tsp. tannin   yeast starter
  1 tablet yeast nutrient   water to 4.55 litre (1 gal.)
Method:
Method A, ignoring all mention of the 'other fruit'. The banana
and honey syrups to be prepared as described in the section on
Ingredients.

(87)

Ingredients:
 1.14 kg. elderberries (2½ lb.)
 226 g. bananas (½ lb.)
 795 ml. red grape concentrate (28 fl. oz.)
 570 g. sugar (1¼ lb.)
 7 g. dried elderflowers
 or 341 ml. elderflowers (12 fl. oz.)
 1½ tsp. malic acid
 1½ tsp. tartaric acid
 1 – 3 mg. Benerva tablet
 1 tablet yeast nutrient
 ½ tsp. ammonium phosphate
 ½ tsp. yeast energiser
 yeast starter
 water to 4.55 litre (1 gal.)

Method:

Method A, ignoring all mention of the 'other fruit'. The banana syrup to be made up as described in the section on Ingredients.

(88)

Ingredients:
 1.14 kg. elderberries (2½ lb.)
 907 g. bilberry pie filling (2 lb.)
 568 ml. red grape concentrate (1 pint)
 795 g. honey (1¾ lb.)
 7 g. dried elderflowers
 or 341 ml. elderflowers (12 fl. oz.)
 1½ tsp. malic acid
 1½ tsp. tartaric acid
 1 – 3 mg. Benerva tablet
 1 tablet yeast nutrient
 ½ tsp. ammonium phosphate
 ½ tsp. yeast energiser
 yeast starter
 water to 4.55 litre (1 gal.)
 2 tsp. Pectozyme

Method:

Method A. The honey syrup to be prepared as described in the section on Ingredients.

(89)

Ingredients:
1.14 kg. elderberries (2½ lb.)
1.14 kg. blackberries, canned (2½ lb.)
568 ml. red grape concentrate (1 pint)
680 g. sugar (1½ lb.)
341 ml. rosepetals (12 fl. oz.)
or 2½ g. dried rosepetals
1½ tsp. malic acid
1½ tsp. tartaric acid
1 – 3 mg. Benerva tablet
1 tablet yeast nutrient
½ tsp. ammonium phosphate   yeast starter
½ tsp. yeast energiser   water to 4.55 litre (1 gal.)
Method:
Method A.

(90)

Ingredients:
1.14 kg. elderberries (2½ lb.)
226 g. figs, canned (½ lb.)
568 ml. red grape concentrate (1 pint)
570 g. sugar (1¼ lb.)
7 g. dried elderflowers
or 341 ml. elderflowers (12 fl. oz.)
1½ tsp. malic acid
1½ tsp. tartaric acid
1 – 3 mg. Benerva tablet
1 tablet yeast nutrient
½ tsp. ammonium phosphate
½ tsp. yeast energiser
yeast starter
water to 4.55 litre (1 gal.)
½ tsp. Pectozyme
Method:
Method A.

(91)

Ingredients:
1.14 kg. elderberries (2½ lb.)
340 g. loganberries, canned (¾ lb.)
226 g. bananas (½ lb.)
710 ml. red grape concentrate (25 fl. oz.)
453 g. sugar (1 lb.)
341 ml. rosepetals (12 fl. oz.)
or 2½ g. dried rosepetals
1½ tsp. malic acid
1½ tsp. tartaric acid
1 – 3 mg. Benerva tablet
1 tablet yeast nutrient   yeast starter
½ tsp. ammonium phosphate   water to 4.55 litre (1 gal.)
½ tsp. yeast energiser   1 tsp. Pectozyme

Method:
Method A. The banana syrup to be prepared as described in the section under Ingredients.

(92)

Ingredients:
1.14 kg. elderberries (2½ lb.)
568 ml. orange juice, unsweetened (1 pint)
426 ml. white grape concentrate (¾ pint)
795 g. sugar (1¾ lb.)
341 ml. rosepetals (12 fl. oz.)
or 2½ g. dried rosepetals
1½ tsp. malic acid
1½ tsp. tartaric acid
1 – 3 mg. Benerva tablet   ½ tsp. yeast energiser
1 tablet yeast nutrient   yeast starter
½ tsp. ammonium phosphate   water to 4.55 litre (1 gal.)

Method:
Method A, ignoring all mention of the 'other fruit'. The orange juice to be added with the grape concentrate:

(93)

Ingredients:
   1.14 kg. elderberries (2½ lb.)
   680 g. peaches, canned (1½ lb.)
   226 g. bananas (½ lb.)
   568 ml. white grape concentrate (1 pint)
   795 g. honey (1¾ lb.)
   7 g. dried elderflowers
   or 341 ml. elderflowers (12 fl. oz.)
   1½ tsp. malic acid
   1½ ts. tartaric acid   ½ tsp. yeast energiser
   1 – 3 mg. Benerva tablet   yeast starter
   1 tablet yeast nutrient   water to 4.55 litre (1 gal.)
   ½ tsp. ammonium phosphate   1½ tsp. Pectozyme
Method:
   Method A. The banana and honey syrups to be prepared as described in the section under Ingredients.

(94)

Ingredients:
   1.14 kg. elderberries (2½ lb.)
   907 g. pears, canned (2 lb.)
   426 ml. white grape concentrate (¾ pint)
   680 g. demerara sugar (1½ lb.)
   7 g. dried elderflowers
   or 341 ml. elderflowers (12 fl. oz.)
   1½ tsp. malic acid
   1½ tsp. tartaric acid
   1 – 3 mg. Benerva tablet
   1 tablet yeast nutrient
   ½ tsp. ammonium phosphate
   ½ tsp. yeast energiser
   yeast starter
   water to 4.55 litre (1 gal.)
Method:
   Method A.

(95)

Ingredients:
   1.14 kg. elderberries (2½ lb.)
   568 ml. pineapple juice, unsweetened (1 pint)
   568 ml. white grape concentrate (1 pint)
   680 g. sugar (1½ lb.)
   7 g. dried elderflowers
   or 341 ml. elderflowers (12 fl. oz.)
   1½ tsp. malic acid
   1½ tsp. tartaric acid
   1 – 3 mg. Benerva tablet
   1 tablet yeast nutrient
   ½ tsp. ammonium phosphate
   ½ tsp. yeast energiser
   yeast starter
   water to 4.55 litre (1 gal.)
   2 tsp. Pectozyme
Method:
Method A, but ignoring all mention of the 'other fruit', and adding the pineapple juice with the grape concentrate.

(96)

Ingredients:
   1.14 kg. elderberries (2½ lb.)
   226 g. prunes, canned (½ lb.)
   568 ml. white grape concentrate (1 pint)
   570 g. sugar (1¼ lb.)
   7 g. dried elderflowers
   or 341 ml. elderflowers (12 fl. oz.)
   1½ tsp. malic acid
   1½ tsp. tartaric acid   ½ tsp. yeast energiser
   1 – 3 mg. Benerva tablet   yeast starter
   1 tablet yeast nutrient   water to 4.55 litre (1 gal.)
   ½ tsp. ammonium phosphate   ½ tsp. Pectozyme
Method:
Method A.

(97)

Ingredients:
1.14 kg. elderberries (2½ lb.)
340 g. raspberries, canned (¾ lb.)
115 g. bananas (¼ lb.)
710 ml. red grape concentrate (25 fl. oz.)
680 g. honey (1½ lb.)
341 ml. rosepetals (12 fl. oz.)
or 2½ g. dried rosepetals
1½ tsp. malic acid
1½ tsp. tartaric acid
1 – 3 mg. Benerva tablet
1 tablet yeast nutrient   yeast starter
½ tsp. ammonium phosphate   water to 4.55 litre (1 gal.)
½ tsp. yeast energiser   1 tsp. Pectozyme
Method:
Method A. The banana and honey syrups to be made as described in the section under Ingredients.

(98)

Ingredients:
1.14 kg. elderberries (2½ lb.)
326 ml. Ribena syrup (11½ fl. oz. bottle)
226 g. bananas (½ lb.)
426 ml. red grape concentrate (¾ pint)
570 g. sugar (1¼ lb.)
7 g. dried elderflowers
or 341 ml. elderflowers (12 fl. oz.)
1½ tsp. malic acid
1½ tsp. tartaric acid   ½ tsp. yeast energiser
1 – 3 mg. Benerva tablet   yeast starter
1 tablet yeast nutrient   water to 4.55 litre (1 gal.)
½ tsp. ammonium phosphate   1 tsp. Pectozyme
Method:
Method A, but ignore all mention of the 'other fruit' and add the Ribena with the grape concentrate, together with the Pectozyme.

PUNCHES

(99)

Ingredients:
1 bottle, 750 ml. (26²/₃ fl. oz.) Wine No. 79
1.14 litre (1 quart) orange juice
¼ tsp. tannin
Caster sugar to taste
Method:
Pour over ice in a bowl and sweeten to taste.

(100)

Ingredients:
1½ bottles, 1.14 litre (40 fl. oz.) Wine No. 74
1 orange
20 cloves
Demerara sugar
Method:
Stick the cloves into the orange, and roll it in the sugar. Roast in a slow oven until moderately browned. Cut up and warm in a saucepan with the wine for ¼ hour, at a temperature not exceeding 74°C (165°F). Strain, when somewhat cooler, into a warmed bowl. Sweeten with the sugar to taste.

(101)

Ingredients:
1 bottle, 750 ml. (26²/₃ fl. oz.) Wine No. 63
20 dashes Angostura Bitters
30 g. (1 oz.) caster sugar
23 cm. (9 in.) stick of cinnamon
3 cloves
5 tsp. allspice
1 lemon, peel only (no pith)

Method:
Put the ingredients into a saucepan, place on a source of heat, and remove at 74°C (165°F). Strain, when cooled a little, into a warmed bowl.

NOTE. Ethyl alcohol boils at 78.5°C (173.3°F), and if the liquors are brought to a higher boiling point, we will be left with the taste of the wine alone, since its alcoholic content will have been lost. For this reason, the use of a preserving thermometer as used in cookery, is well worth the trouble involved.

CUPS & COOLERS

(102)

Ingredients:
1 bottle, 750 ml. (26²/₃ fl. oz.) Wine No. 74
1.14 litre (1 quart) mineral water
1 lemon
113 g. (¼ lb.) caster sugar
25 mm. (1 in.) length of cucumber
1 leaf borage
1 orange
1 tbsp. raspberry syrup

Method:
Pour the wine into a large jug, add the peel of the orange (no pith) and the juice of the orange and of the lemon. Stir in the sugar and the raspberry syrup. Add the thinly sliced cucumber and the borage leaf. Keep in the refrigerator until required, then add the mineral water. Serve with ice cubes.

(103)

Ingredients:
1½ bottles, 1.14 litre (1 quart) Wine No. 5
1 bottle, 500 ml. (17.6 fl. oz.) soda water
3 lemons
1 saltspoonful nutmeg
113 g. (¼ lb.) caster sugar
mixed fresh fruit to taste

Method:
Put the juice of the lemons, and the peel (no pith) from one lemon, into a jug, stir in the sugar and the grated nutmeg; leave covered for 2 hours. Strain through fine nylon into a large jug, add the wine, stir in the soda water, and garnish with mixed fresh fruit in season. Serve with ice cubes.

(104)

Ingredients:
   2 bottles, 1.14 litre (1 quart) Wine No. 79
   2 bottles, 1 litre (35.2 fl. oz.) soda water
   568 ml. (1 pint) tea
   2 lemons
   4 oranges
   113 g. (¼ lb.) sugar
Method:
Use fresh tea; strain (if not using a teabag) over the sugar contained in a large jug, and stir to dissolve. Cover, and leave to cool. Add the juice of the lemons and oranges, followed by a few ice cubes. Add the wine and soda water just before serving. Garnish with sliced oranges and lemons, together with a sprig of mint.

(105)

Ingredients:
   1 bottle, 750 ml. (26²/₃ fl. oz.) Wine No. 36
   1 can, 570 g. (1 lb. 4 oz.) pineapple chunks
   2 tbsp. caster sugar
   12 strawberries
   1 bottle, 500 ml. (17.6 fl. oz.) soda water
Method:
Put the pineapple in a bowl, together with the strawberries, sugar and wine; keep in the refrigerator. Pour in the soda water just before serving.

CORDIALS

(106)

Ingredients:
1.14 litre (1 quart) elderberry juice
453 g. (1 lb.) sugar
7 g. (¼ oz.) cloves
7 g. (¼ oz.) cinnamon
2 nutmegs
¼ bottle, 199 ml. (7 fl. oz.) brandy

Method:
Gradually stir in the sugar whilst heating up the juice, and skim off the scum after boiling point has been reached; add the cloves, cinnamon and grated nutmeg, and keep at simmering point for half-an-hour. Cover, and leave to cool. Funnel the brandy into a quart bottle, add the juice (which will have decreased in volume whilst simmering) to fill the bottle, and stopper securely.

(107)

Ingredients:
453 g. (1 lb.) elderberries
28 g. (1 oz.) cloves
28 g. (1 oz.) root ginger
1 kg. (2.2 lb.) sugar
½ tsp. malic acid
½ tsp. tartaric acid
1 – 3 mg. Benerva tablet   ½ tsp. yeast energiser
1 tablet yeast nutrient   yeast starter
½ tsp. ammonium phosphate   water to 4.55 litre (1 gal.)

Method:
This is the same as for the Aperitif, Table and Social wines previously described – Method 1A. The spices in the recipe can be changed to produce a range of alcoholic cordials such as have been produced in England since Anglo-Saxon times. Some alternatives are aniseed, cinnamon, lovage and peppermint.

WINE COCKTAILS

(108)

Ingredients:
  Wine No. 68
  1 cube sugar
  angostura bitters
  lemon peel
Method:
  Put the lump of sugar into a cocktail glass (capacity 85 ml. – 3 fl. oz.) and soak it with angostura bitters. Add three squeezes of lemon juice. Top up with the ice-cold wine, and garnish with a small piece of lemon peel (no pith).

(109)

Ingredients:
  Wine No. 64
  1 orange
  orange peel
  Wine No. 66
Method:
  Put equal parts of the wines into a cocktail glass, 28 ml. (1 fl. oz.) each, add the juice from the orange, and garnish with a piece of the orange peel (no pith).

(110)

Ingredients:
  Wine No. 70
  Orange bitters
Method:
  Three parts fill the cocktail glass with the wine, and add a couple of dashes of orange bitters.

VERMOUTHS

These are drinks made from wine of about 17% alcoholic content by volume (30° proof) which have had the essence of herbs added; wormwood, a bitter herb, is usually the basic additive, and the other herbs used modify this bitterness and provide other distinctive characteristics; angelica and gentian are well known in this respect.

Other wine aperitifs make use of cinnamon, cloves, coriander, nutmeg, orange and orris root in the same manner.

French and Italian vermouth flavourings are available from home-winemaking stores, and should be used according to the instructions provided.

Fluid extracts of many herbs are available from Health Food shops, and provide scope (see above) for experimentation. Wormwood, angelica and gentian are useful in this category.

If fresh or dried herbs, and/or spices are used, they are contained in a nylon bag and immersed in the wine until the desired degree of flavour has been attained.

A wine which has disappointed so far as flavour is concerned, can provide the basis for these herb and spice additives.

A good purpose-made basic wine recipe is as given hereunder, and is made in accordance with the Dessert wine Method C:

(111)

Ingredients:
907 g. black-violet elderberries (2 lb.)
or green (ripe) elderberries
710 ml. red grape concentrate (25 fl. oz.)
or white grape concentrate
795 g. sugar (1¾ lb.)
1 tsp. malic acid
1 tsp. tartaric acid
1 – 3 mg. Benerva tablet
1 tablet yeast nutrient
½ tsp. ammonium phosphate
½ tsp. yeast energiser
yeast starter
water to 4.55 litre (1 gal.)

LIQUEURS

Liqueurs are normally served in small glasses of about 85 ml. (3 fl. oz.) capacity, into which about 57 ml. (2 fl. oz.) are poured.

The reaction to a taste of any particular liqueur is usually either favourable or unfavourable – there is little room for indifference.

For this reason, and because of the cost involved, we will use 241 ml. (8.5 fl. oz.) screw-top bottles on our production line. Each bottle will thus provide a drink each for four people. These mixer-drink bottles can be made quite attractive in appearance with the aid of different coloured enamels applied to the screw-tops in conjunction with suitable labels.

We're not trying to reproduce commercial liqueurs here, although similarities must occur when home-winemaking liqueur flavourings are used, except that we will not be using a neutral-flavoured wine, which will give added interest to the end product. Commercial liqueurs vary in strength, but an alcoholic content of 50° proof (28.5% by volume) is a fair average, and should win general approval, and a chance of maintaining sobriety, if needful – or added ability to enjoy more drinks.

The wine given hereunder, which will ferment out to an alcoholic content of 30° proof (17% by volume) will be used for all our liqueurs.

Vodka at 70° proof will provide the additional alcohol requirement.

Eight saccharin (Sweetex) pellets per bottle will provide the anticipated degree of sweetness.

The final ingredient is the flavouring, which will not amount to more than a small part of the remaining space in the bottle, leaving room for shaking.

Hence our liqueur formulation is:

(112)

114 ml. vodka 70° proof (4 fl. oz.)
114 ml. wine 30° proof (4 fl. oz.)
8 saccharin (Sweetex) pellets
flavouring essence

Our wine will be produced in accordance with the Dessert wine Method C, ignoring all references to the 'other fruit'.

(113)

Ingredients:
1.36 kg. green (ripe) elderberries
or black-violet elderberries
907 g. bananas (2 lb.)
795 ml. white grape concentrate (28 fl. oz.)
or red grape concentrate
625 g. sugar (22 oz.)
2 tsp. malic acid
2 tsp. tartaric acid
1 – 3 mg. Benerva tablet
1 tsp. tannin (for green elderberries only)
1 tablet yeast nutrient
½ tsp. ammonium phosphate
½ tsp. yeast energiser
yeast starter
water to 4.55 litre (1 gal.)

Some flavouring essences available from home-winemaking shops are: ananas, anise, apricot brandy, cacao, cherry brandy, cichona, coffee rum, curacao, creme de menthe, danzig, dictine, green convent, green mint, grenadine, honey smoke, kernel, kummel, mandarine, maraschino, mirabelle, orange, peach brandy, prunelle, ratafia, reverendine; they are usually added by drops, and in such case an eye-dropper comes in useful.

From supermarkets, flavouring essences such as almond, brandy, chocolate, coffee, peppermint and rum are readily available. Your taste buds will probably appreciate one teaspoonful per bottle, but brandy and rum flavours may well run to a full 2 teaspoonfuls.

BONUS WINES

The before-given formulations contain from 453 to 1360 g. (1 to 3 lb.) of elderberries per 4.55 litre (gallon) of wine. The value of the elderberries for winemaking will in no way be exhausted after one extraction. It is fully practicable to make three separate 4.55 litres (gallons) of wine from 1.36 kg. (3 lb.) of elderberries by means of a second and then a third use of the same batch of fruit:

(114)

Ingredients:
1.36 kg. elderberries, second extraction (3 lb.)
710 ml. red grape concentrate (25 fl. oz.)
570 g. sugar (1¼ lb.)
1 tsp. malic acid
1 tsp. tartaric acid
1 – 3 mg. Benerva tablet   ½ tsp. yeast energiser
1 tablet yeast nutrient   yeast starter
½ tsp. ammonium phosphate   water to 4.55 litre (1 gal.)
Method:
As Method A, ignoring all mention of 'other fruit'.

(115)

Ingredients:
1.36 kg. elderberries, third extraction (3 lb.)
795 g. sugar (1¾ lb.)
½ tsp. malic acid
½ tsp. tartaric acid
1 – 3 mg. Benerva tablet
1 tablet yeast nutrient
½ tsp. ammonium phosphate
½ tsp. yeast energiser   water to 4.55 litre (1 gal.)
yeast starter   1 tsp. Pectozyme
Method:
As Method D, ignoring all mention of 'other fruit'.

The Pectozyme is used to increase the extraction from the elderberries, and the pulp fermentation is continued until the required depth of colour is attained in each case; usually a maximum of three days.

The permutations and combinations which are available in this re-use of the elderberries are almost endless, and the above-given formulations are intended only to illustrate the possibilities.

SERVING

After all the time and care spent on producing your wine, don't slip up at the final hurdle and fail to present it to its best advantage. It can be made unpleasant to drink due to preservative and maturation gases not having had the opportunity to escape, and the bouquet can be improved if attention is paid to a few small details.

Still white wines benefit when transferred to a decanter an hour before required for drinking, and the taste is more pleasant when they are served freshly chilled at about 10°C (50°F). The bouquet will suffer by a prolonged stay in the refrigerator.

Still red wines should also be in the decanter for an hour before drinking, but red dessert wines benefit by half a day so disposed. They are best served at 18°C (65°F).

Sparkling wines must, of course, be served direct from the bottle. They are best served at about 7°C (45°F), ideally from an ice bucket, but a short stay in the refrigerator answers the purpose. Do not serve from the freezer after disgorgement (described earlier), or the bouquet, taste and sparkle will suffer thereby. Hold the bottle at an angle when removing the wire and stopper, and keep it that way whilst pouring into the glasses, which are best grouped together to minimize spillage.

The wine in the glass should have eye-appeal to enhance its enjoyment. This calls for brightly polished, plain, clear glasses, of a capacity suitable for their purpose. The bouquet of the wine is another pre-drinking pleasure not to be lost; this calls for tulip-shaped glasses curved inward toward the top, so as to retain the bouquet. Sparkling wines should be served in tall, similarly-shaped glasses, so that not only the bouquet, but the bubbles also are retained as much as possible; the old-fashioned shallow champagne glasses lose out on both counts, and are to be avoided.

INDEX